my **revision** notes

OCR AS/A-level History

ENGLAND 1485–1558

THE EARLY TUDORS

Nicholas Fellows

HODDER
EDUCATION
AN HACHETTE UK COMPANY

Every effort has been made to trace all copyright holders, but if any have been inadvertently overlooked, the Publishers will be pleased to make the necessary arrangements at the first opportunity.

Although every effort has been made to ensure that website addresses are correct at time of going to press, Hodder Education cannot be held responsible for the content of any website mentioned in this book. It is sometimes possible to find a relocated web page by typing in the address of the home page for a website in the URL window of your browser.

Hachette UK's policy is to use papers that are natural, renewable and recyclable products and made from wood grown in sustainable forests. The logging and manufacturing processes are expected to conform to the environmental regulations of the country of origin.

Orders: please contact Bookpoint Ltd, 130 Milton Park, Abingdon, Oxon OX14 4SE. Telephone: +44 (0)1235 827720. Fax: +44 (0)1235 400454. Email education@bookpoint. co.uk Lines are open from 9 a.m. to 5 p.m., Monday to Saturday, with a 24-hour message answering service. You can also order through our website: www.hoddereducation.co.uk

ISBN: 9781 4718 7597 7

© Nicholas Fellows 2017

First published in 2017 by
Hodder Education,
An Hachette UK Company
Carmelite House
50 Victoria Embankment
London EC4Y 0DZ
www.hoddereducation.co.uk

Impression number   10 9 8 7 6 5 4 3 2 1

Year   2021 2020 2019 2018 2017

Cover photo © Chris Dorney/Alamy Stock Photo
Illustrations by Integra
Typeset in Bembo Std Regular 10.75/12.75 by Integra Software Services Pvt. Ltd., Pondicherry, India
Printed in Spain

A catalogue record for this title is available from the British Library.

My Revision Planner

Enquiry Topic: Mid Tudor Crises, 1547–58

REVISED

Introduction

Unit 1: British Period Study and Enquiry

Unit 1 involves the study of a period of British history. At both A and AS-level there are two sections to the examination. Section A is the Enquiry section and Section B is the Essay section. In the Enquiry section there will be four primary written sources and one question for the A-level examination, and three primary written sources and two questions for the AS-level. Section B will consist of two essays, of which you will have to answer one. The type of essay set for both AS and A-level are similar, but the AS mark scheme does not have a level 6 (see page 7).

The Early Tudors: 1485–1558

The specification lists the content of the Period Study element, which is England 1485–1547, under four Key Topics:
- Key Topic 1 – The government of Henry VII and threats to his rule.
- Key Topic 2 – Henry VII's foreign policy.
- Key Topic 3 – Henry VIII and Wolsey.
- Key Topic 4 – The reign of Henry VIII after 1529.

The specification lists the content of the Enquiry element, which is the Mid Tudor Crises 1547–58, under three Key Topics:
- Key Topic 1 – The stability of the monarchy, 1547–58.
- Key Topic 2 – Religious changes, 1547–58.
- Key Topic 3 – Rebellion and unrest, 1547–58.

Although each period of study is set out in chronological sections in the specification, an exam question may arise from one or more of these sections.

AS-level

The AS-level examination which you may be taking includes all the content.

You are required to answer the following:
- Section A: two questions. They are source-based questions and will require you to use your knowledge to explain, analyse and evaluate three primary sources. The first question will require you to consider the utility of one of the sources for a particular issue and is worth 10 marks. The second question will require you to explain, analyse and evaluate the three sources in relation to an issue and is worth 20 marks. The section is worth 30 marks.
- Section B: one essay question from a choice of two. The essays require you to explain, analyse and assess an issue, using your knowledge to reach a balanced judgement about the question. The question is worth 20 marks.

The exam lasts one and a half hours, and you are advised to spend slightly more time on Section A.

At AS-level, Unit 1 will be worth a total of 50 marks and 50 per cent of the AS-level.

A-level

The A-level examination at the end of the course includes all the content.

You are required to answer the ONE question from Section A and ONE essay from Section B from a choice of TWO questions:
- Section A is the Enquiry question and will contain four written primary sources. You will be asked to use the four sources to test a hypothesis by considering the provenance and content of the sources and applying your own knowledge to the sources to reach a judgement about the sources in relation to the issue in the question. This is the same as the AS-level Question 2 but uses four sources instead of three.
- The essay questions are similar in style and requirement to the AS-level essay question, except to reach the highest level you will need to show a more developed sense of judgement.

The exam lasts for one and a half hours. You should spend slightly longer on Section A than B.

At A-level, Unit 1 will be worth a total of 50 marks and 25 per cent of the A-level.

AS-level

In both the AS and A-level examinations you are being tested on:
- your ability to use relevant historical information
- the skill of analysing factors and reaching a judgement.

In the AS-level examination you are also being tested on your ability to analyse and evaluate the different ways in which aspects of the past have been interpreted.

How to use this book

This book has been designed to help you develop the knowledge and skills necessary to succeed in the examination. The book is divided into seven sections – one for each section of the AS and A-level specifications. Each section is made up of a series of topics organised into double-page spreads.
- On the left-hand page you will find a summary of the key content you will need to learn.
- On the right-hand page you will find exam-focused activities.

Together these two strands of the book will provide you with the knowledge and skills essential for examination success. Words in bold in the main content are defined in the glossary (see pages 99–100).

▼ **Key historical content**

▼ **Exam-focused activities**

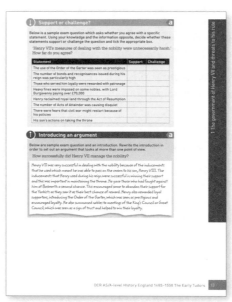

Examination activities

There are three levels of exam-focused activities:
- **Band 1** activities are designed to develop the foundation skills needed to pass the exam. These have a green heading and this symbol:
- **Band 2** activities are designed to build on the skills developed in Band 1 activities and to help you to achieve a C grade. These have an orange heading and this symbol:
- **Band 3** activities are designed to enable you to access the highest grades. These have a purple heading and this symbol:

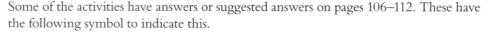

Some of the activities have answers or suggested answers on pages 106–112. These have the following symbol to indicate this.

Each section ends with exam-style questions and sample answers with commentary. This will give you guidance on what is expected to achieve the top grade.

You can also keep track of your revision by ticking off each topic heading in the book, or by ticking the checklist on the contents page. Tick each box when you have:
- revised and understood a topic
- completed the activities.

Mark schemes

For some of the activities in the book it will be useful to refer to the mark schemes for this paper. Below are abbreviated forms.

AS-level

Level	Question 1 Utility	Question 2 All three sources	Question 3 or 4 Essay
5	Good focus, evaluation using provenance and context to engage with the issue to reach an analysis of its utility. **9–10**	Good focus, sources are evaluated using provenance and context, although there may be some imbalance, to reach an analysis of the issue. **17–20**	Mostly focused, supported answer with good analysis and evaluation to reach a supported judgement. **17–20**
4	Mostly focused, evaluated using provenance and context, with some imbalance to engage with the issue to reach an analysis of its utility. **7–8**	Mostly focused, sources are evaluated using some provenance and context to reach an analysis of the issue. **13–16**	Some focus with support, analysis with limited evaluation and judgement. **13–16**
3	Partial focus and evaluation of either context or provenance to produce a partial analysis of its utility. **5–6**	Partial focus and evaluation, some context to produce a partial analysis of the issue. **9–12**	Partial focus on the question, with some knowledge and analysis, but little or no judgement. **9–12**
2	Limited focus, general or stock evaluation to produce a limited analysis of the issue. **3–4**	Limited focus, evaluation is general as is context. General analysis of the issue. **5–8**	Focus is descriptive and may be more on the topic than the question. Any analysis may be implied. **5–8**
1	Answer is on the topic, basic evaluation and general knowledge. Simple or general analysis of the issue. **1–2**	Answer is on the topic, basic evaluation, much description of the sources and general contextual knowledge leading to a simple analysis of the issue. **1–4**	Focus on the topic and attempts at analysis will be little more than assertion. **1–4**

A-level

Level	Source question	Essay
6	Well focused, sources are fully evaluated using provenance and context to reach a fully supported analysis of the issue. **26–30**	Well focused, supported answer with very good analysis and developed evaluation to reach a supported and sustained judgement. **17–20**
5	Good focus, sources are evaluated using provenance and context, although there may be some imbalance, to reach an analysis of the issue. **21–25**	Mostly focused, supported answer with good analysis and evaluation to reach a supported judgement. **13–16**
4	Mostly focused, sources are evaluated using some provenance and context to reach an analysis of the issue. **16–20**	Some focus with support, analysis with limited evaluation and judgement. **10–12**
3	Partial focus and evaluation, some context to produce a partial analysis of the issue. **11–15**	Partial focus on the question, with some knowledge and analysis, but little or no judgement. **7–9**
2	Limited focus, evaluation is general as is context. General analysis of the issue. **6–10**	Focus is descriptive and may be more on the topic than the question. Any analysis may be implied. **4–6**
1	Answer is on the topic, basic evaluation, much description of the sources and general contextual knowledge leading to a simple analysis of the issue. **1–5**	Focus on the topic and attempts at analysis will be little more than assertion. **1–3**

1 The government of Henry VII and threats to his rule

Henry's claim

Henry Tudor defeated the **Yorkist** King, Richard III, at the Battle of Bosworth in August 1485. He would go on to rule England as King **Henry VII** until his death in 1509 and pass the throne on securely to his son, who became **Henry VIII**.

Although Henry was the male **Lancastrian** claimant to the throne, his claim was poor and was likely to be challenged by Yorkist claimants (see page 10) who had seen their King killed at Bosworth.

Henry's claim to the throne was very weak, being largely through his mother, Margaret Beaufort, who was a descendant of Edward III by the marriage of his third son, John of Gaunt, to Catherine Swynford. However, the children had been born when Catherine was John's mistress and were legitimised later by parliament.

Henry did have some royal blood as his father's mother was a French princess who had been married to Henry V before marrying Owen Tudor, Henry's grandfather.

This weak claim meant that Henry held the throne because he had defeated Richard and not because he was the legitimate ruler.

Henry's weak position

Henry was also in a weak position. He had spent fourteen years in exile after the Lancastrians were defeated at Tewkesbury in 1471. This meant that he was largely unknown and therefore many might assume that it would be foolhardy to support him as his reign was unlikely to last.

Strength of Henry's position

Despite Henry's weak claim, there were strengths to his position:
- Richard III had been unpopular, particularly as it was rumoured that he had killed the 'Princes in the Tower' – the children of Edward IV – in order to take the throne.
- The country was weary of war after the **Wars of the Roses** and therefore might support Henry if he could offer peace and stability.
- Richard III was dead, as were many Yorkists with a better claim, as was shown by the use of 'Pretenders' (see page 10).
- Henry had not depended upon another noble family to help him take the throne.

The importance of Bosworth

Although Henry's position was strengthened because the previous King, Richard III, had been killed, it did not give him the support of the country. Many nobles remained neutral during the battle, as they disliked Richard III, but it did not necessarily mean that they would support Henry.

Henry was aware of his weak position and took a series of actions to help strengthen it:
- He dated the start of his reign from the day before Bosworth so that those who had fought against him were traitors. This meant they could have their land seized, which would increase Henry's wealth.
- His coronation was on 30 October, before parliament met, so that it could not be claimed he was King only because of them.
- He asked for **papal dispensation** to marry Elizabeth of York, a distant cousin, to unite the houses of Lancaster and York.
- The marriage took place after he was crowned so it could not be claimed he owed the throne to his wife.
- Henry was willing to give Yorkists who had supported Richard at Bosworth a second chance, with the **Duke of Northumberland** restored to his old position to control the north. This encouraged other Yorkists to support Henry.

Spectrum of significance

Below are a sample exam question and a concluding paragraph written in answer to this question. Annotate the paragraph to develop the argument as to which factor was the most significant.

> Assess the reasons why Henry VII's position as King of England was so weak.

There were many reasons why Henry VII's position on the throne of England was so fragile, but the main reason was his weak claim to the English throne, which could be challenged by Yorkist claimants, even though their King had been killed at Bosworth. Though there were other reasons, these were less important. Henry had been in exile for fourteen years and this meant that he was largely unknown. Many might assume that it would therefore be foolhardy to support him as it was likely that his reign would be short-lived. Although Richard had been killed at Bosworth, it did not mean that the country supported Henry, similarly although many nobles remained neutral during the battle it did not mean they would throw their power behind the new King. Richard may have murdered the 'Princes in the Tower', but there were other Yorkists who could challenge Henry — just because he had won at Bosworth did not mean that the 'Wars of the Roses' were over.

Turning assertion into argument **a**

Below are a sample exam question and a series of assertions. Read the question and then add a justification to each of the assertions to turn it into an argument.

> To what extent was Henry VII able to strengthen his position as King of England in the period to the end of 1486?

Henry's marriage was important in strengthening his position on the throne:

_____

_____

People were tired of the instability caused by the Wars of the Roses:

_____

_____

The death of Richard at Bosworth strengthened Henry's position:

_____

_____

The Yorkists were weak:

_____

_____

Henry's skills allowed him to strengthen his position:

_____

_____

Yorkist opposition

Although the Wars of the Roses had killed many Yorkists with a claim to the throne, there were still two of Richard's nephews, Edward, Earl of Warwick, and John de la Pole, Earl of Lincoln, who had strong claims. Warwick was soon removed as a threat by being sent to the Tower of London and Lincoln professed loyalty and was invited to join the **King's Council**. However, there were still others who were willing to challenge Henry's position. The Yorkists also found that they had support from overseas, particularly from **Margaret of Burgundy,** who was the sister of Edward IV and Richard III.

Lovell and Stafford

Within a year of taking the throne Henry faced unrest. Lord Lovell and the Stafford brothers (Humphrey and Thomas) had been loyal supporters of Richard and attempted to raise a rebellion in the Midlands and north in the spring of 1486, but it failed because Henry had spies who brought it to his knowledge. Lovell fled to Flanders and the Staffords sought sanctuary. Humphrey was executed, but Thomas was pardoned. Henry's progress to the north also helped to win him loyalty.

The threat of the Pretenders

The lack of Yorkist claimants should have increased Henry's security, but instead they found suitable candidates who could impersonate one of the Princes in the Tower and this led to Simnel's rising in 1487 and Warbeck's from 1491–99.

Simnel's rising

Lambert Simnel claimed to be one of Richard III's nephews, the Earl of Warwick, and his rising was a major threat as it came within a year of Henry taking the throne and forced the King into battle, which could easily have had a similar result to Bosworth. The rising had begun in the autumn of 1486, but Henry was not aware of it until 1487. Simnel was crowned Edward VI in Ireland, and received support from Margaret of Burgundy and the Earl of Lincoln. However, when the rebels landed in Lancashire they failed to attract support and this was not helped by the presence of Irish, who were seen as brutal, among the force. Henry paraded the real Earl of Warwick and raised an army which confronted Simnel at Stoke near Newark. Although some of his men held back, Henry was successful.

Perkin Warbeck

Perkin Warbeck claimed to be Richard, Duke of York, one of the Princes murdered in the Tower, and therefore Henry could not parade the real Prince. The origins of the conspiracy are unclear and although the rising was not a direct threat, it lasted a long time and had international support from France and Burgundy. Warbeck first appeared in Ireland, but gained little support. He was welcomed at the French court but when Henry signed the **Treaty of Étaples** (see page 22) he moved to Flanders. Although he also had the support of the Holy Roman Emperor, he was more concerned about Italy and Henry was able to act. Warbeck landed at Deal in 1495 and was driven away by the militia. He went to Ireland and failed to win support, but was welcomed in Scotland and married James IV's cousin. He invaded from the north, but again got little support and on returning to Scotland was abandoned by the King. He attempted another invasion of England in the west to coincide with the Cornish rising (see page 14), but this failed and he gave himself up in 1497. He remained at court, but further plotting resulted in his execution in 1499.

The latter years and security

The final Yorkist challenge came from Edmund de la Pole, but in 1506 Philip of Burgundy was persuaded to hand him over. Therefore, although it had taken much of his reign, it can be argued Henry was finally secure. However, the death of his wife and eldest son, Arthur, did weaken his position and meant the Tudor dynasty's survival depended upon Henry's other son surviving.

Below are a sample exam question and the first paragraph of an answer. Why is this not likely to lead to a high mark? Once you have identified why, rewrite the paragraph.

How serious a threat to Henry VII was the Yorkist challenge?

> The Yorkist threat to Henry was serious at the start of his reign for many reasons. The new King's position was weak and there were a number of Yorkists with a claim who were able to appeal to the people and take advantage of Henry's position. They were able to raise support from outside England as well as within the country. There were also Pretenders who were able to raise support and challenge Henry because his position was weak, although he was easily able to defeat them, suggesting they were less of a threat. All these reasons help to explain why the Yorkist threat was, at least at the start of Henry's reign, serious.

Simple essay style

Below is a sample essay question. Use your own knowledge, information on the opposite page and information from other sections of the book to produce a plan for the question. Choose four general points, and provide three specific pieces of information to support each general point. Once you have planned your essay, write the introduction and conclusion for the essay. The introduction should list the points to be discussed in the essay. The conclusion should summarise the key points and justify your argument.

Assess the reasons why the Yorkists failed to defeat Henry VII.

Introduction:

_____

_____

_____

Point 1:

_____

_____

Point 2:

_____

_____

Point 3

_____

_____

Point 4:

_____

_____

Conclusion:

_____

_____

_____

_____

Relations with the nobility

The nobility were seen as a problem as they had caused, at least in part, the Wars of the Roses in 1450s and 1460s. There was also nothing stopping another powerful noble overthrowing Henry. Given both their power and wealth it was vital that Henry controlled them, although historians disagree as to how great a threat they were. The nobility were vital to Henry as:

- he needed their help and advice to rule
- he needed them to enforce royal will in the localities
- they were required to fill key offices.

Control of the nobility

Henry used two methods to control the nobility: the 'carrot' and the 'stick', or inducements and sanctions.

Inducements

- Henry gave many who fought against him at Bosworth a second chance.
- He established the **Order of the Garter**, which was seen as prestigious.
- He gave patronage in return for loyal service, not in the hope of loyal service – nobles had to *prove* they were loyal.
- He issued summons to the King's Council, which was a sign of trust.

Sanctions

- **Acts of Attainder** damaged families as they lost the right to possess land, thus bringing social and economic disaster on a family. They could be reversed as a result of good behaviour.
- The use of bonds and recognisances; these were written agreements whereby nobles who had offended the King paid him money or paid money as security for future behaviour. This discouraged potentially disloyal nobles.
- Limits were placed on noble **retainers**; they needed a licence to keep retainers and this was followed by a heavy fine if not kept. Lord Burgavenny was fined over £70,000.
- Henry asserted his feudal rights over marriage, profiting from the arranged marriage of heirs and by exploiting the estates of wards.
- Henry also took back former royal land, seen with the Act of Resumption in 1486. This made the King wealthier and therefore more powerful than any other noble.

It is difficult to argue that his actions were not successful in controlling the nobility:

- There was little noble unrest after the defeat of Simnel.
- The number of over-mighty subjects was reduced.
- The number of new nobles created was limited and therefore elevation was seen as a great privilege.

However, by the end of Henry's reign the increase in the number of Acts of Attainder, which reached 51 in the period 1504–09, was causing disquiet. Similarly 36 out of 62 noble families were involved in bonds and recognisances, which according to one historian were 'a terrifying system of suspended justice'.

It is therefore not surprising that some have argued that civil war might have broken out again had Henry not died in 1509, such was the harshness of the methods he was employing. Therefore, despite having five times more land than Henry VI, his position was still not secure. Having taken the throne by force there was no reason why another noble could not successfully challenge his rule and remove him. Certainly his son's actions when he came to the throne suggest that there was a need to restore good relations with the nobility if the Crown and Tudor dynasty was to be secure.

Support or challenge? a

Below is a sample exam question which asks whether you agree with a specific statement. Using your knowledge and the information opposite, decide whether these statements support or challenge the question and tick the appropriate box.

'Henry VII's measures of dealing with the nobility were unnecessarily harsh.' How far do you agree?

Statement	Support	Challenge
The use of the Order of the Garter was seen as prestigious		
The number of bonds and recognisances issued during his reign was particularly high		
Those who served him loyally were rewarded with patronage		
Heavy fines were imposed on some nobles, with Lord Burgavenny paying over £70,000		
Henry reclaimed royal land through the Act of Resumption		
The number of Acts of Attainder was causing disquiet		
There were fears that civil war might restart because of his policies		
His son's actions on taking the throne		

Introducing an argument a

Below are sample exam question and an introduction. Rewrite the introduction in order to set out an argument that looks at more than one point of view.

How successfully did Henry VII manage the nobility?

Henry VII was very successful in dealing with the nobility because of the inducements that he used which meant he was able to pass on the crown to his son, Henry VIII. The inducements that Henry used during his reign were successful in winning their support and this was important in maintaining the throne. He gave those who had fought against him at Bosworth a second chance. This encouraged some to abandon their support for the Yorkists as they saw it as their best chance of reward. Henry also rewarded loyal supporters, introducing the Order of the Garter, which was seen as prestigious and encouraged loyalty. He also summoned nobles to meetings of the King's Council or Great Council, which was seen as a sign of trust and helped to win their loyalty.

Royal finances

Strong royal finances were important if Henry VII was to secure the throne and they would allow him to raise forces to put down unrest and provide his son with money to secure the throne against challengers. Henry attempted to strengthen royal finances in three ways:

- reorganisation of financial administration
- exploiting sources of ordinary revenue
- increasing income from extraordinary revenue.

Opposition to taxation in Yorkshire and Cornwall

Increasing income created opposition from those who were forced to pay, as the King was expected to 'live off his own' and this was seen in two taxation revolts.

Yorkshire tax revolt, 1489

This started because Henry needed to raise money to aid Brittany against France. The northern counties objected as they were usually exempt from tax because of the cost of defending the northern border from the Scots. Henry did not negotiate and the tax collector, the Earl of Northumberland, was murdered. The rising was easily crushed, but no tax was collected as Henry recognised the need to compromise.

The Cornish rising, 1497

This was more serious, but was caused by the same factors. Henry wanted the west to pay towards the invasion from the north by Warbeck (see page 10). The rebels gathered at Bodmin and marched to London before they were crushed at Blackheath by a royal army of 25,000. The rising attracted 15,000 men and although it was not a threat to Henry, the leaders were executed and others fined.

Financial administration

In the Middle Ages monarchs used the Exchequer to administer crown finance, but it was slow. Edward IV had used the chamber system. At first Henry went back to the Exchequer, but by 1487 he realised it was inefficient and went back to the chamber system, which dealt with all income except customs duties. This increased the importance of the Treasurer of the Chamber and Gentlemen of the Bedchamber, but it gave Henry greater control.

Ordinary revenue

This came from crown lands, customs, justice and feudal dues. The amount of income varied each year. The most important source of revenue was the ownership of crown lands and Henry ensured this increased:

- The 1486 Act of Resumption restored crown lands.
- Lands were taken from those who were attainted (i.e. the families lost the right to possess land).
- Income from the duchy of Lancaster increased ten-fold.

Henry skilfully exploited the crown lands to increase his income. However, he was less successful with customs and was unable to match Edward IV's £70,000 per annum, with customs income dropping to £40,000 because of smuggling and international relations influencing trade. Henry exploited the justice system, using fines rather than imprisonment to raise money. Income from feudal dues rose dramatically as he enforced his rights, increasing from £350 in 1487 to £6000 in 1507.

Extraordinary revenue

The most frequent source was parliamentary taxation, but it was expected it would be raised only at times of emergency, and even then it caused opposition. The amount raised varied and was limited because it was based on out-of-date assessment figures. Henry also asked wealthy subjects for loans and **benevolences**; the latter were not repaid and therefore could not be used regularly. He also raised money from the Church and levied money through feudal aid to fund occasions such as the knighting of his son, Arthur.

Henry has been accused of being greedy. He ran a lavish court in order to maintain an image of power and prestige. Income had risen to £113,000 per year and the Crown was again solvent by 1509.

! Delete as applicable a

Below are a sample question and a paragraph written in answer to this question. Read the paragraph and decide which of the possible options (in bold) is most appropriate. Delete the least appropriate options and complete the paragraph by justifying your selection.

'Henry VII's financial policy was a great success.' How far do you agree?

Henry VII's financial policy was a great success to a **limited/fair/great extent**. He was able to increase **all/some/most** areas of ordinary revenue. He was particularly **successful/unsuccessful** with customs, which **increased/decreased** in comparison to the reign of Edward IV. His exploitation of revenue from crown lands was a **limited/fair/great** success and this was **similar to/different from** his exploitation of the justice system. However, raising money through extraordinary revenue was **more/less** successful as he was expected to use it **regularly/infrequently/in times of emergencies** and using this method was **popular/unpopular** and it provided a **regular/variable/limited** income.

_____

_____

_____

⚡ Identify an argument a

Below are a series of definitions, a sample exam question and two sample conclusions. One of the conclusions achieves a high level because it contains an argument (an assertion justified with a reason). The other achieves a lower level because it contains only description (a detailed account) and assertion (a statement of fact or an opinion, which is not supported by a reason). Identify which is which.

How serious was the opposition to Henry VII's financial policies?

CONCLUSION 1

Though there was some opposition to his financial policies, in the form of taxation rebellions, it did not prevent Henry from leaving the Crown solvent. The Cornish rising did attract large numbers and was able to reach London before it was crushed, but it never seriously threatened Henry's position and was able to draw on the support of only one noble, Lord Audley. Although the Yorkshire rising did result in the death of the tax collector, the rising never left the region and like the Cornish rising was easily crushed. However, the more serious threat to his financial policy came from the nobles who disliked his exploitation of the system of bonds and recognisances which left many in financial penury and, according to some accounts, was close to bringing England to civil war, suggesting that his financial exploitation of the nobility was a greater threat than his attempts to levy taxation.

CONCLUSION 2

There were two tax revolts in this period, the Yorkshire rising in 1489 and the Cornish rising in 1497. The risings complained about the financial demands placed on the region, with Yorkshire objecting to fund a war against France, while the Cornish refused to pay to defend the Scottish border. The risings were crushed, but Henry did recognise the need to compromise with the rebels, although with the Cornish rising the leaders were executed and others fined.

Henry VII and administration

The Wars of the Roses had done much to destroy 'good government' and although there was some restoration during Edward IV's second reign (1471–83) and under Richard III (1483–85), Henry was determined law and order would be firmly established.

Central government

Although Henry was King, he needed advice and he could not rule alone. The Council was the most important element. Henry relied on an inner group of councillors, which made meetings more efficient. It included:

- Morton, the Lord Chancellor
- Fox, the Lord Privy Seal
- Dynham, the Lord Treasurer
- and five other members.

He also used smaller committees within the Council, including the Court of Requests and Council Learned in the Law, which handled bonds and recognisances (see page 12). Most members of the Council were from the nobility or Church, but some important members came from the gentry. He used lesser landowners, gentry and professional classes, particularly lawyers, for his chief advisors. **Royal rights** were increasingly exploited and this led to hatred towards men such as Richard Empson and Edmund Dudley, who played important roles in enforcing bonds and recognisances.

Regional government

Henry developed the Yorkist system of regional councils in outlying areas where royal authority was less strong.

Council of the North

This not only defended the border with Scotland, but had administrative and judicial power so the law was enforced quickly. Henry appointed its members so they were loyal and enforced royal will, appointing Surrey after the Yorkshire rising.

Council of Wales

This was re-established in 1493, following the model used by Edward IV. It was under the ruling of his son Arthur, but Henry used his Welsh connections and the death and loss of lands by Marcher lords to increase control.

Ireland

This was a problem because of its support for Yorkists. Direct royal control was limited to the Pale, around Dublin. Attempts to bring Ulster under control failed and because of the cost Henry was forced to rely on rule by the traditional families, such as Kildare.

Local government

This had often broken down during the Wars of the Roses, with many noble families building up power blocs. Henry wanted to ensure his laws were enforced, but did not have paid officials to do this and so had to rely on the nobles and gentry to uphold his wishes. Henry was content for this to happen, but also developed the existing office of **Justice of the Peace (JP)**. He chose men from the lesser nobility and gentry who were therefore more likely to be loyal as they did not have the power of the great nobles; this also weakened the power of the greater nobles. The role of JPs was increased to include imposing economic and social statutes, dispensing justice, upholding order, rewarding informers and arresting poachers. However, many were unwilling to act as it made them unpopular.

Parliament

Parliament was not a permanent feature of government. The King could summon, **prorogue** and dissolve it when he wanted. It met only seven times during his reign, but was used to pass Acts of Attainder and to uphold his claim to the throne. Most meetings were brief because:

- Henry wanted to avoid asking for money as it caused disquiet
- Henry avoided war
- most Acts of Attainder were at the start or end of his reign
- parliament's role as a law court was taken up by the Council Learned in the Law.

Much had been done to improve law and order by the end of his reign, although Henry still relied on goodwill and a willingness to implement the laws.

ⓘ Complete the paragraph

a

Below are a sample exam question and a paragraph written in answer to the question. The paragraph lacks a clear point at the start, but does contain supporting material and an explanatory link back to the question at the end. Complete the paragraph by writing in the key point at the start. Use the space provided.

To what extent was Henry VII able to restore law and order in England?

_____

_____

_____

This point is supported by his reliance on unpaid officials. The use of JPs was not new, but Henry increased their role and this now included imposing economic and social laws and dispensing justice. However, they were unpaid officials and were concerned that they did not become unpopular in the localities, but by choosing men from the second rank of society they were more likely to be loyal and carry out the King's wishes. Despite their role, Henry still needed the support of the nobility to ensure that laws were implemented in the localities, and regional councils to enforce law and order in the peripheral regions were equally important. Thus the explanation cannot be totally one-sided.

ⓘ Spider diagram

Use the information on the opposite page and your own knowledge to add detail to the spider diagram below to identify some of the methods used by Henry to govern England.

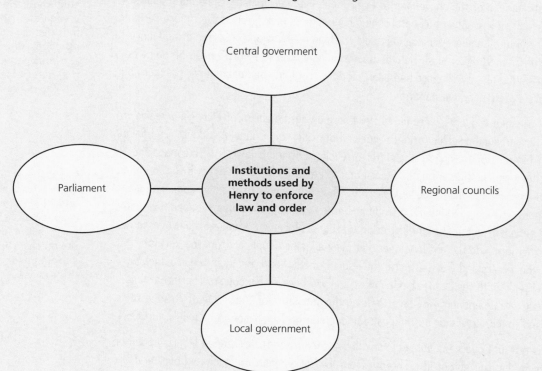

Exam focus

Below are an exam-style question and high-level model answer. Read them and the comments around the answer.

How serious were the challenges to Henry VII?

Although Henry's position in 1485 was insecure he passed the throne on to his son following his death in 1509, suggesting that the challenges he faced were not that serious. His claim to the throne was weak and there were challenges to his position, particularly in the early years of his reign. However, these were not only overcome but declined over time. The most serious challenge came from the Yorkists who had been defeated at Bosworth, but even they were reduced to using Pretenders to try and regain their power. Many nobles, accustomed to the unrest of the Wars of the Roses, had become tired of instability and were willing to support the new King once it became apparent he was able to restore order, further reducing his challenges.

> The opening paragraph offers a view and some ideas as to why the challenges were not serious and declined.

Henry's greatest challenge was his weak claim to the throne. Although Richard III had usurped the throne and probably killed Edward IV's children, Henry VII's claim was largely based on his victory at Bosworth, rather than legitimacy. This meant that there was little stopping others attempting to claim the throne. Even though he was the Lancastrian claimant, his claim was not strong as it was through his mother, Margaret Beaufort. She was a descendant of Edward III by the marriage of his third son, John of Gaunt, to Catherine Swynford, but this link to royal blood was weakened as the children had been born when Catherine was John's mistress and had to be legitimised later by parliament. Yet, even with this claim, and his later marriage to Elizabeth of York, it was always likely that he would be challenged by Yorkists who had seen their King killed.

> A threat is identified and analysed and a judgement reached. The material is linked back to the question set.

The seriousness of the challenges to Henry was made very clear in the early years of his rule when Henry was still establishing his position, making the threat more serious. The Pretender, Lambert Simnel, was able to raise an invasion force and bring Henry to battle at East Stoke. The battle was a serious challenge to Henry's position as he could have been beaten, as Richard had been, and his front line had been under pressure by Simnel's experienced mercenaries.

> The paragraph explains why Simnel posed a serious challenge, there is some detail about the battle and a judgement reached. As with the previous paragraph the material is linked back to the question.

The challenges to Henry were made more serious by the ability of Henry's enemies to raise foreign support. The Yorkists received considerable financial and military backing from Margaret of Burgundy, the sister of Richard III and Edward IV. This made the challenge particularly serious as Henry could ill afford bad relations with Burgundy as it was the centre for the English wool trade. The seriousness of the challenge was made very apparent when, in 1493, a trade embargo with Burgundy was imposed because of its support for the Pretender Perkin Warbeck. However, it was not just overseas support that made the challenge serious, Simnel gained support from the Yorkist stronghold in Ireland. Furthermore, the courts of Scotland and France gave backing to Warbeck, with the Scottish King marrying Warbeck to his cousin. The threat was deemed serious enough for Spain to delay the departure of Catherine of Aragon to England to marry Arthur as they were uncertain the Tudor monarchy would survive.

> The issue of foreign support is considered and a judgement reached as to how serious it made the threat. The seriousness of the threat is assessed.

It was not just overseas support for other claimants that threatened Henry's position, but from the English nobility. Threats from the Yorkist nobility, such as Lovell and Stafford in 1486, were potentially serious as Henry was not secure on the throne. Many nobles, such as Northumberland and Norfolk, were still powerful and had become accustomed to ruling as virtual kings, often ignoring royal will. They were a serious threat, seen most clearly when Stanley, supposedly a loyal supporter of Henry, supported Warbeck. Despite his efforts, Henry was not secure from the Yorkist threat until 1506 when Philip of Burgundy handed over Suffolk. Despite this apparent triumph for Henry, his policies of bonds and recognisances and attainders had alienated many, which has led some to argue that Henry was fortunate to avoid a noble rebellion in the last years of his reign. However, many nobles did support Henry and were willing to take advantage of the rewards that their loyalty brought, while others were controlled through Henry's extensive spy network, which had helped to defeat the threat from Lovell and Stafford in 1486, suggesting that he was more secure than the unrest initially indicated.

His position was strengthened by the lack of genuine Yorkist claimants, while others were willing to accept the second chance Henry gave them and prove their loyalty. His position was further enhanced as Richard had been killed at Bosworth and so, along with the death of Edward IV's children, could not provide a focus for opposition. Such was the weakness of the Yorkist threat that they had to turn to the Pretenders Simnel and Warbeck. While the former was able to bring Henry to battle, Warbeck was not a serious threat, more a nuisance, as his attempts at invasion at Deal in 1495 and in the West Country in 1497 were a fiasco, with him driven from Deal by the local militia and forced to seek sanctuary in 1497.

> There is a balanced discussion of the threat from the Yorkists and nobility and an overall assessment is made.

Although Henry faced two taxation rebellions from Yorkshire in 1489 and Cornwall in 1497, these were not a threat as the complaints were about the levying of taxes and did not challenge Henry's position as King and were easily crushed. Even though the Cornish rising was able to raise 15,000 men and reach Blackheath it was still easily crushed and would have been dealt with earlier if not for the Warbeck rising.

> Although the paragraph is short, the seriousness of the challenge is analysed.

Although Henry's position was weak in 1485 and the early challenges had the potential to remove him, he was not only able to survive but to strengthen his position. Recognition from foreign powers, such as Spain, suggest his position was secure. In 1487 Henry was not secure as a Pretender had been able to bring him to battle, but by 1497 Warbeck was unable to seriously threaten the King, was easily driven from both Taunton and Exeter and forced to give himself up. The challenges in the early years were serious, but declined as the reign progressed and Henry became more secure.

> The overall judgement continues the line of argument outlined in the opening paragraph and some support is provided for that judgement so that it is not simply asserted.

The answer remains focused throughout, with the material linked back to the question set. There are judgements made at the end of each paragraph, although in some areas they could be further developed. The line of argument remains constant and the conclusion follows logically from the rest of the essay.

Reaching a judgement

In order to reach the very top level candidates need to reach judgements about the issues they are considering in relation to the question. Identify those paragraphs in the answer above where the candidate has done this successfully and those where a judgement is either absent or not developed. In the latter case write a couple of sentences for each of the paragraphs so that a judgement based on the argument is reached.

2 Henry VII's foreign policy

Henry VII's aims

England was not a major power in 1485. It had lost the **Hundred Years War** with France in the 1450s and it lacked a **standing army**. It was vulnerable to attack in the north from Scotland and across the Channel from France.

Henry VII was in an insecure position because of the Yorkist threat and his weak claim. As a result his foreign policy was subordinate to achieving internal security and to securing his throne from foreign threats. As a usurper he also wanted foreign recognition, while his financial position, which was weak at the start, made him vulnerable and needing to avoid war. However, he was able to use foreign policy to strengthen his position through alliances and marriages.

Threat of invasion

There was not just a threat of invasion from other claimants, but also from foreign powers, such as Scotland and France, who might exploit Henry's weak position. This was made a greater threat as France and Scotland were allies through the **Auld Alliance**. In the early years he therefore secured truces with both so that he could consolidate his position at home. Although these truces did not last he was later able to develop alliances and agreements with them.

Dynastic threats

The Yorkist challenge, which was his greatest threat, was not confined to home, but was actively encouraged by Margaret of Burgundy. Henry therefore needed to improve relations with the major powers and gain allies. Henry subsequently sought to make an alliance with Spain which would give him protection, recognition and a guarantee that they would not support other claimants; this was sealed through the marriage of Arthur to **Catherine of Aragon** in 1501. Similarly, an agreement was eventually reached with Scotland through the Peace of Ayton, which led to the marriage of Henry's daughter, Margaret, to James IV.

Financial position

Given Henry's weak financial position it was important to avoid war. War was costly and he lacked the funds. However, war also occupied the nobles and prevented them causing unrest at home. When he did go to war against France in 1492 it was at the end of the campaigning season and France was more concerned about developments in Italy, with the result that the French King restored the **French pension** with the Treaty of Étaples and also promised not to support Henry's opponents (see page 22).

Economic aims

Henry was concerned with improving England's economic position as increased revenue from trade would strengthen the monarchy. Henry was therefore keen to maintain the cloth trade with Burgundy and develop closer trading relations with other powers. However, trade was of secondary importance to national security and the cloth trade with Burgundy was suspended when they supported Warbeck. Trade agreements were signed with other countries, including Brittany, Spain and Florence.

Henry's foreign policy can be conveniently divided into three phases:
- 1485–92: A period of diplomacy when Henry's main concern was to secure the throne.
- 1493–1502: A period when peace with Scotland was secured and Henry's position appeared stronger.
- 1503–09: A less successful period as Henry became more isolated.

Spectrum of significance

Below are a sample exam question and a list of general points, which could be used to answer it. Use your knowledge and the information on the page opposite to reach a judgement about the relative importance of the factors. Write numbers on the spectrum below to indicate their relative importance. Having done this, write a brief justification of your placement on the line, explaining why some of these factors are more important than others. The resulting diagram could form the basis of an essay plan.

'Henry VII's most important foreign policy aim was to secure the Tudor dynasty.' How far do you agree?

1   The threat of invasion from France

2   The threat of invasion from Scotland

3   Secure the Tudor dynasty

4   Gain recognition from European powers

5   Avoid costly wars

6   Improve foreign trade

←——————————————————————————————→

Least important   Most important

Reasons behind your placement:

_____

_____

_____

_____

_____

_____

Eliminate irrelevance
a

Below are a sample exam question and a paragraph written in answer to the question. Read the paragraph and identify the parts that are not directly relevant to the question. Draw a line through the information that is irrelevant and justify your deletions in the margin.

Assess the aims of Henry VII's foreign policy.

Henry had numerous foreign policy aims and his policy can be divided into three distinct phases. In the first part of his reign from 1485 to 1492 Henry's main concern was to secure his throne. During this period he followed a policy of diplomacy in order to win support, while at home he also tried to eliminate those who could threaten his throne, crushing unrest and limiting the power of the nobility. In the period from 1493 to 1502 it appears that Henry's main concern was to secure peace with Scotland, which was done through the Treaty of Ayton. This also helped him to secure his throne as it helped in the defeat of Warbeck. In the last period of Henry's reign his aim was to ensure that he was not isolated overseas as England was still relatively weak. He was also faced with a declining position at home with the death of his wife and eldest son, so his aim at home was to ensure the Tudor dynasty survived.

Relations with France and Scotland

These two countries were the biggest threat to Henry. Scotland bordered England in the north and France was England's traditional enemy and had the largest and most professional army in Europe, added to which the two were long-standing allies and so could launch a joint invasion.

France

The Brittany affair

France had given Henry financial aid when he took the throne, but they were also keen to take Brittany, which was a threat to England as it would place all the Channel coast in French hands. Henry's position was made more difficult when Brittany asked for English help. However, England could not aid Brittany alone and when Maximilian, the Holy Roman Emperor, made peace with France, Brittany was forced to accept defeat and the ruler of Brittany, Anne, married Charles VIII of France. Henry had agreed to send 6,000 soldiers to aid Brittany, but there was now a danger of attack from France.

War with France

Henry, like English Kings before him, asserted his claim to the French throne. He gathered an invasion force and launched this in October 1492. However, the timing meant the campaigning season was nearly over and France was more concerned by events in Italy. France therefore soon offered peace and the Treaty of Étaples was signed whereby the countries agreed that:

- France would not aid English rebels, particularly Warbeck.
- France would pay the arrears from the **Treaty of Picquigny**.
- France would pay most of Henry's expenses for aiding Brittany.
- Henry would gain a French pension of £5,000 per year, about 5 per cent of his income.

Relations with France after 1492

The League of Venice, established in 1495 to drive France out of Italy, initially excluded England, but when it became the Holy League in 1496 England was added. However, England was not committed to go to war against France and could stay neutral. At the same time, Henry also signed a trade deal with France, suggesting he had done well as he was included in the alliance but kept his friendship with France.

Henry tried to develop this with a three-way agreement between England, France and the Netherlands against Spain, and it appeared to be successful with the 1508 League of Cambrai. However, just before it was due to be signed France withdrew as they did not want to antagonise Spain, and France then joined with Spain, leaving England isolated.

Scotland

Scotland was the traditional enemy and the border region was the site of regular conflict and skirmishes. Although Scotland was much weaker than England, it was allied to France and this made it more of a threat. Initially relations appeared to improve, but the coming of age of James IV in 1495 changed the situation.

Scotland and Warbeck

James wanted to assert himself against England by going to war and this was made easier by the arrival of Warbeck in 1495. Warbeck was married to the King's cousin and given military aid. However, Warbeck's invasion was a fiasco. James therefore took up the offer of peace and this led to Warbeck's departure and the signing of Truce of Ayton in 1497, which became a full peace in 1499.

Improvement in relations

This was the first peace agreement between England and Scotland since 1328. It led to the marriage of Henry's eldest daughter, Margaret, to James IV in 1503, which gave Henry further recognition. It prevented full-scale war for the rest of Henry's reign, but there were still skirmishes and Scotland did not abandon its alliance with France.

You're the examiner **a**

Below are a sample exam question and a paragraph written in answer to this question. Read the paragraph and the mark scheme provided on page 7. Decide which level you would award the paragraph. Write the level below along with a justification for your decision.

How successful was Henry VII's foreign policy towards France and Scotland?

Henry VII's policy towards France and Scotland was mostly successful. France and Scotland were England's traditional enemies and their alliance meant that they were a serious threat to England as they could attack from both the northern border and the Channel coast. However, apart from Henry's decision to go to war with France in 1492, it was short-lived and he was able to avoid war with both countries. Despite this success, there were still border skirmishes with Scotland. Henry was able to sign England's first peace agreement with the Scots since 1328 and cement the improved relations with the marriage of his eldest daughter to James IV. This was also successful as Scotland abandoned its support for Warbeck and gave Henry recognition from another European power. Henry was not as successful in his dealings with France as he failed to prevent the annexation of Brittany, which placed the whole of the Channel coast in French hands. Although he gained financially from the Treaty of Étaples that ended the 1492 war, he was unable to secure France as an ally at the end of his reign when he attempted to arrange a three-way agreement between England, France and the Netherlands, ultimately leaving England isolated. Therefore, although border skirmishes continued with Scotland, Henry was more successful in securing the northern border with Scotland than he was in arranging a treaty with France.

Level:

Reason for choosing this level:

_____

_____

 Recommended reading

Below is a list of suggested further reading on this topic:
- *England 1485–1603*, pages 30–50, Mary Dicken and Nicholas Fellows (2015)
- *England and Europe, 1485–1603*, pages 12–22, Susan Doran (1986)
- *Henry VII*, pages 125–42, Caroline Rogers and Roger Turvey (2005)
- *The Early Tudors*, pages 37–56, D. Rogerson, S. Ellsmore and D. Hudson (2001)

Relations with Burgundy and Spain

Burgundy and Spain played central roles in Henry's foreign policy. Burgundy was important for two reasons:

- It was the centre of the cloth trade and England depended upon it for exports.
- It had become a centre for Yorkists because of the presence of Margaret of Burgundy.

Meanwhile, Spain had become more united because of the marriage of the rulers of the kingdoms of Aragon and Castile, Ferdinand and Isabella. This marriage had created a new European power and Henry wanted to strengthen ties with them both in terms of trade and dynastic concerns. This aim was made easier as they shared a common enemy in France.

Relations with Burgundy

Good relations with Burgundy were crucial, but they were not easy because of the safe haven given to Yorkists and the support to the Pretenders, Simnel and Warbeck. Despite the cloth trade, Henry VII prioritised national security and therefore placed an embargo on trade with Burgundy between 1493 and 1496 when they supported Warbeck. It ended with the Magnus Intercursus (see page 28).

Relations improved in 1506 when Philip of Burgundy was forced to seek shelter from a storm in England and wanted support against Aragon. Henry was able to negotiate a more favourable commercial treaty, Malus Intercursus (see page 28), and persuaded Philip to hand over the Yorkist Earl of Suffolk, who was sheltering in Burgundy. Henry feared Burgundy would support the Earl in an attempt to seize the English throne. Handing him over eliminated the final Yorkist threat.

A pro-Burgundian alliance appeared to have been formed at the expense of the alliance with Spain. To pursue the alliance with Burgundy, Henry revoked the Malus Intercursus as it was too favourable to English merchants. However, the alliance did not succeed as the other prospective member, France, abandoned it to avoid antagonising Spain. He also made a marriage agreement with Archduke Charles, the son of Philip, to marry Henry's daughter, **Mary Tudor**.

Relations with Spain

For much of his reign Henry sought to improve relations with the new great power in Europe. In 1488 Henry proposed a marriage between Arthur and Catherine of Aragon, the youngest daughter of Ferdinand and Isabella. This would give Henry recognition from a major power and signify they considered him secure on the throne. Although negotiations were slow the Treaty of Medina del Campo was signed in 1489:

- Arthur and Catherine were to marry.
- Catherine's **dowry** was £40,000, to be paid in instalments.
- Spain would not help English rebels.
- Trade was to be improved.
- Each would help the other in a war against France.

Spain wanted to regain lands in the Pyrenean region, but Henry was more concerned in gaining recognition. The final marriage agreement was not signed until 1496 and Catherine did not arrive until 1501, in part because Spain was concerned by the threat from Warbeck.

Improved relations with Spain did not last following the death of Isabella in 1504 and the subsequent succession crisis, which lasted until 1506. Henry moved towards a Burgundian alliance as Philip of Burgundy claimed Castile for his wife, Joanna, Isabella's daughter. This meant that the marriage to Catherine had less appeal and ensured that policy in the last years of Henry's reign was more confused and made more difficult because of improved relations between France and Spain, which meant that Spain did not need English friendship. However, the death of Philip ended his attempts to claim Castile, which was retaken by Ferdinand. This recovery of power made the Spanish marriage more attractive again for England and, following Arthur's death, Henry pursued a marriage for his second son, Henry, to Catherine. Ferdinand did not agree to this and by 1508 Henry had abandoned Spain and moved towards an anti-Spanish alliance.

Complete the paragraph **a**

Below are a sample exam question and a paragraph written in answer to the question. The paragraph contains a point and specific examples, but lacks a concluding explanatory link back to the question. (Remember that 'assess the reasons' involves more than explaining some reasons.)

Assess the reasons why the Treaty of Medina del Campo was so important to Henry VII.

> The Treaty of Medina del Campo was a reflection of Henry's concern to obtain foreign recognition and that he needed the support of major European powers in order to secure the Tudor dynasty on the throne, which was still threatened by Pretenders, such as Perkin Warbeck, who could threaten the King's position. The treaty included an agreement that Spain would not support other claimants to the English throne. Henry wanted to secure a valuable marriage for his son, which would strengthen England's position within Europe and stop them from appearing to be a second-rate power, which had been their position since the ending of the Hundred Years War with France. The treaty would also signify that Ferdinand and Isabella of Spain considered Henry secure enough on the throne to allow their daughter to marry into the Tudor family. The treaty also contained trade clauses and Henry hoped that these would give England access to lucrative markets. The importance of the treaty can be explained both in terms of recognition for the Tudors and strengthening English security, and improving trade.
>
> _____
>
> _____

 Simple essay style

Below is a sample exam question. Use your own knowledge and information on the opposite page and pages 22, 26 and 28 to produce a plan for the question. Choose four or five general points, and provide three pieces of specific information to support each one. Once you have planned your essay, write the introduction and conclusion for the essay. The introduction should list the points to be discussed in the essay. The conclusion should summarise the key points and justify which point was the most important.

'Henry VII's greatest foreign policy achievement was the alliance with Spain.' How far do you agree?

Marriage negotiations

Marriage agreements played a crucial role in Henry's foreign policy. They helped gain foreign recognition for the Tudors and they also provided allies, further strengthening their position and helping to provide dynastic security.

Marriage agreements with Spain

The marriage agreement with Spain, signed in 1489, was important for Henry as not only was his eldest son, Arthur, to marry Catherine of Aragon, but it also gave the Tudors recognition from a major European power.

Its importance was reinforced by Henry's decision to celebrate it by minting a new gold sovereign on which he was portrayed wearing an imperial crown, suggesting he considered his position more secure. However, the final marriage agreement was not signed until 1496 and Catherine did not come to England until 1501 because of the Warbeck threat.

Henry also hoped to use the marriage to gain access to the new Spanish empire; and because Catherine's sister, Joanna, had married Philip of Burgundy, he also hoped to use the marriage to bring about an alliance with Burgundy.

The value of the marriage was made even clearer when, with Arthur's death just five months after the marriage, Henry suggested that Catherine should marry his second son, Henry. The King did not want to lose the alliance and, after a papal dispensation was obtained, Catherine was betrothed to Henry in 1503, but it was only after Henry VII's death that the marriage took place. Moreover, Henry VII angered Ferdinand by keeping the dowry and Catherine and not proceeding with the marriage agreement.

Marriage agreements with Scotland

Marriage was also used to improve relations with one of England's traditional enemies, Scotland. Following Scottish support for Warbeck, James IV feared that England might attack Scotland and therefore when Henry offered terms on which a treaty could be based, they were accepted.

The truce that was signed became the Peace of Ayton in 1499 and one of the terms was the marriage of Henry VII's eldest daughter, Margaret, to James IV, which took place in 1503. The marriage brought Henry recognition from another European state and reinforced his position on the throne. Although it did not prevent border skirmishes, it did prevent full-scale war breaking out again in his reign.

Failed marriage agreements

Towards the end of his reign Henry attempted a number of other marriage agreements.

Death of Queen Elizabeth

With the death of his own wife in 1503, Henry considered the possibility of re-marrying. Marriage to Joanna of Naples, Margaret of Savoy and Joanna of Castile were attempted in turn. Marriage to Joanna of Naples was encouraged by Spain as she was Ferdinand's niece and he wanted to strengthen his alliance with England against France, but the death of Isabella of Castile ended the proposal. Margaret of Savoy rejected the proposal as she wanted to remain a widow. Henry then sought to marry Joanna of Castile, to maintain the English, Spanish and Burgundian alliance against France. However, Ferdinand, who had now allied to France, refused and also failed to send the rest of Catherine's dowry.

Marriage of Mary

In 1507 the Holy Roman Emperor, Maximilian, agreed to Archduke Charles, the son of Philip of Burgundy and Joanna of Castile, marrying Henry's younger daughter, Mary, but this did not take place.

Henry tried again to win the hand of Margaret of Savoy and then, to annoy the Spanish, he offered his surviving son as a husband to Louis XII's niece, Margaret of Angouleme.

Marriage agreements were used initially to gain recognition and improve security. However, in the latter part of Henry's reign marriage negotiations reflected the changing direction of English foreign policy and Henry's attempts to create alliances which strengthened the realm.

(i) The flaw in the argument   a

Below are a sample exam question and part of an answer to it. Identify the flaw in the argument and suggest how the answer could be improved. Write your answers below.

'The achievements of Henry VII's marriage agreements were limited.' How far do you agree?

> The marriage agreements of Henry VII achieved little because Arthur died and the marriage of Margaret to James IV did not end border skirmishes or make the border with Scotland any more secure. The marriage agreement with Spain was crucial to Henry's desire for recognition and this is made clear by the fact that when Arthur died Henry was quick to suggest that his other son, Henry, marry Catherine. Although this occurred only after Henry VII's death, it did secure the alliance. Not only that, but Henry was also able to increase national security as Spain agreed not to help English rebels and trade between the two nations was also to be improved, further supporting the argument that the marriage agreement was a success. Similarly with Scotland the agreement was a success as it was the first peace treaty between the two nations since 1328 and did help to prevent full-scale war from breaking out until his son's reign.

The flaw is:

_____

The paragraph could be improved by:

_____

_____

(i) Turning assertion into argument   a

Below are a sample exam question and a series of assertions. Read the exam question and then add a justification to each of the assertions to turn it into an argument.

How successful were Henry VII's marriage agreements in increasing dynastic security?

Henry VII's marriage agreement with Spain was successful in increasing dynastic security:

_____

_____

However, the success was only short-lived because:

_____

_____

Similarly the marriage agreement with Scotland was only partially successful because:

_____

_____

Trade agreements

Although national security was the most important factor influencing Henry's foreign policy, he did promote trade whenever possible because of the financial benefits that it brought both England and the monarchy. However, given England's relatively weak position, he was not usually strong enough to offer favourable trade terms to other countries and was forced to react to events. Yet this did not mean that he did not give consideration to the impact his foreign policy would have on trade and many agreements, as with Spain in the Treaty of Medina del Campo, included trade clauses.

Trade with Burgundy: Magnus Intercursus and Malus Intercursus

The main focus of English trade was with Burgundy because of the importance of the cloth trade through Antwerp. Henry wanted to increase the amount of trade, but figures suggest it stayed the same throughout his reign. However, despite its importance it remained secondary to national security, as was seen when an embargo was enforced between 1493 and 1496 because of Burgundian support for Perkin Warbeck and merchants were ordered to move their trade to Calais.

The embargo was ended by the Magnus Intercursus in 1496. This allowed English merchants to sell their goods anywhere in Philip's lands, except Flanders, without paying tolls or customs.

Henry exploited the situation in 1506 when storms forced Philip to seek shelter in England, signing the Malus Intercursus, which gave English merchants considerable advantages:
- Trade with Burgundy would be free.
- Philip was not to impose any duties on the sale of English cloth.
- Philip was not to exclude English cloth from his lands.
- Philip's subjects had to pay the duties outlined in the Magnus Intercursus.

The terms were very favourable to English merchants and annoyed Burgundy so much that in 1507 the Magnus Intercursus was restored.

Agreements with other countries

Henry used other treaties to try and improve England's trading position.

Trade with Spain

Henry had initially confirmed the Spanish privilege of exemption from duties payable by other foreigners on the import of English goods. However, he then imposed the Navigation Acts in 1485–86, which limited foreign control of English trade. Spain retaliated and forbade the export of goods from Spain in foreign ships.

The Treaty of Medina del Campo resolved the problems:
- Both countries had the same rights in each other's countries.
- Duties were fixed at a low rate.

However, Spain did not give England access to the New World, although English trade did develop in the Mediterranean, in part because of the Italian Wars.

Other agreements

- An earlier trade treaty with Portugal was renewed. (Portugal was England's oldest ally – the first treaty was made in the fourteenth century.)
- A commercial treaty was signed with Brittany in 1486.
- A trade agreement was reached with Florence in 1490 and an English staple was established at Pisa.

After Antwerp, the Baltic was probably England's most important trading area. The trade was dominated by the Hanseatic League and Henry attempted to limit their privileges through the Navigation Acts, but this failed. Henry also tried to improve the position of English merchants there by signing treaties with Denmark and Norway in 1489 and 1490, and then Riga in 1499. As with the Navigation Acts, this policy was not successful and the Hanse's favourable position was restored, in part because Henry was worried that they might support Yorkist claimants, suggesting that once again dynastic security was his major concern.

Spot the mistake

Below are a sample exam question and a paragraph written in answer to the question. What mistake is stopping the paragraph being of a high quality? Rewrite the paragraph so that it displays the qualities of at least Level 5. The mark scheme is on page 7.

'Henry VII's main foreign policy aim was to improve trade.' How far do you agree?

Henry VII was concerned with promoting trade because of the financial benefits it would bring both England and the monarchy. The issue of national security was a concern to Henry and treaties often contained agreements that other nations would not protect Henry's enemies. As a usurper, Henry also wanted to gain foreign recognition and this was an aim of his foreign policy, which he attempted to achieve through marriage agreements with other powers. As England was weak Henry was also concerned with securing allies to help strengthen both his position and increase national security.

 ## Introducing an argument

Read the following sample exam question, a list of key points to be made in the essay, and a simple introduction and conclusion for the essay. Rewrite the introduction and conclusion in order to develop an argument.

To what extent was Henry VII able to improve English overseas trade?

Key points:

- Many treaties contained trade clauses
- Trade was secondary to national security
- Trade with Burgundy, because of cloth, was England's priority
- Henry used trade embargoes when security was threatened
- The Treaty of Medina del Campo resolved many trade issues with Spain
- Henry was unable to improve trading relations with the Hanse

Introduction:

There were some ways in which Henry VII was able to improve English trade. Henry was able to sign treaties with a number of countries that helped to improve England's trading position. There were also times when actions that Henry took did not improve trade. There were threats to national security and Henry had to deal with those. England was not particularly strong and this also made it difficult for Henry to improve trade.

Conclusion:

Thus we may see that there were times when treaties signed with other countries meant that trade was improved. Henry was able to obtain favourable trading terms with some countries. However, there were occasions when actions that Henry took did not improve trade. National security was important and Henry had to ensure the realm was safe.

2 Henry VII's foreign policy

Exam focus

Below are an exam-style question and a high-level answer. Read them and the comments around the answer.

How successful was Henry VII's foreign policy?

Henry VII's position as King was very insecure because of his weak claim to the throne and the Yorkist threat. As a result his foreign policy was closely linked to ensuring that he retained the throne. He faced the threat of invasion from other claimants and from England's traditional enemies, France and Scotland. There was also the possibility that other European rulers might exploit his weak claim to undermine him or, in the case of Burgundy, to restore the Yorkist line. Therefore his main concerns were to stop invasion and secure his dynastic position and the success of his foreign policy should be judged against these major concerns. Henry also inherited a weak financial position and therefore wanted to avoid costly wars. Linked to this was the desire to increase trade as that would increase revenue and therefore strengthen the monarchy. However, when national security was threatened, trade would become a secondary consideration.

> The opening paragraph establishes Henry's aims, a set of criteria against which success can be judged.

There can be little doubt that Henry was successful in preventing invasion. Neither France nor Scotland launched a major attack against England. France was more concerned about the struggles in Italy and Charles signed the Treaty of Étaples in 1492, which included the agreement not to aid English rebels. Furthermore, Scotland in the early part of Henry's reign was ruled by a minor following the death of James III in 1488. Although James IV, once he came of age, gave support to Warbeck and wanted to launch an invasion of England, he realised that Warbeck lacked support and he would be better accepting the terms Henry offered. The Truce of Ayton, which later became a full peace treaty following the death of Warbeck, secured the northern border for Henry and was reinforced through the marriage of Henry's eldest daughter, Margaret, to the Scottish King. This was a considerable achievement as no peace treaty had been signed between the two countries since 1328. Although there were still occasional border raids and the Auld Alliance between France and Scotland was not broken, there was no invasion. However, Henry had been unable to prevent the French from annexing Brittany in 1491 and this gave France control of much of the Channel and a potential base from which to launch an invasion. Therefore, although on the surface he was more secure from invasion, the potential threat was still there.

> A clear view is offered.

> The view is supported and a judgement is reached.

Henry was also largely successful in dealing with the threat to dynastic security. Through both marriage agreements and treaties he was able to win recognition for the Tudor dynasty. The most significant achievement was the Treaty of Medina del Campo with Spain in 1489. This not only gained Henry recognition from the rising European power, but also included an agreement for Henry's eldest son, Arthur, to marry Catherine of Aragon. However, although the treaty was signed in 1489 she did not arrive in England until 1501, suggesting that Spain was unwilling to allow her to come to England until they were certain Henry was secure and the threat from Warbeck had been extinguished. Moreover, the death of Arthur within a few months of the marriage and the dispute over the Castilian inheritance following the death of Isabella weakened the agreement, although Henry did arrange for his second son to marry Catherine. The most serious threat to Henry's dynastic security was from Burgundy, where Margaret of Burgundy, sister of the former King, Richard III, supported Yorkist claimants and provided aid to both Warbeck and Simnel. Burgundy was also important as the major

> Another of Henry's aims is considered and a range of issues are discussed before a judgement about the issue is reached.

Quick quizzes at **www.hoddereducation.co.uk/myrevisionnotes**

centre of trade for English cloth. Henry was initially less successful in his policy towards Burgundy as he was forced to place an embargo on trade between 1493 and 1496 following the support given to Warbeck. It was only in 1506 when Philip of Burgundy was forced to seek shelter in England that Henry was able to improve his security by forcing Philip to sign a treaty in which he agreed to hand over the Yorkist claimant, the Earl of Suffolk. Therefore, although Henry had been able to improve his security it was not without its difficulties and it was only towards the end of his reign that the potential threat from Burgundy was nullified.

Henry was able to use his foreign policy to help improve his financial position. Although his weak financial position meant that he wanted to avoid war, he did go to war against France in 1492. This was successful as not only did it increase his credibility at home following the failure to prevent the annexation of Brittany, but it also occupied the nobility and resulted in a very favourable peace treaty. Henry was clever in that the invasion was launched at the end of the campaigning season so no major battle took place and, with Charles more concerned with Italy, Henry negotiated a favourable peace. This re-established the French pension, which brought in £5,000 per year, but also resulted in France agreeing to pay the arrears from it, further boosting Henry's income. He was also successful in avoiding war with Scotland as, having raised a force to invade Scotland, the Scots, fearing defeat, agreed to peace.

> A further aim is examined and there is a clear argument linking back to the question, but a judgement about the success is missing.

Henry did improve trade, but only when it did not threaten security. He was able to win a very favourable trade agreement with Burgundy, the Malus Intercursus, when Philip sought refuge, but this was only short-lived because it was favourable to England, but not to Burgundy. However, he was able to restore the Magnus Intercursus which had been signed in 1496, which allowed English merchants to sell their goods wholesale anywhere in Philip's lands, except Flanders, without paying tolls. He was also able to sign trade agreements with Portugal and Florence, but his attempt to limit the power of the Hanseatic League did fail.

> As with the previous paragraph, an issue is analysed with detailed support, but a judgement is lacking.

Although much of his foreign policy was a success, the last years did see a weakening of England's position. Henry's attempt to negotiate a marriage agreement for himself with a variety of European powers failed and Spain and France reached an agreement, which became the League of Cambrai, from which England was excluded. However, although England was isolated at the end of Henry's reign, there was no significant threat to the Tudor succession or of invasion, perhaps in part because the major conflict was in Italy where England had little interest. Aware of England's limited power, he was able to secure his position and gain recognition through a series of marriages and treaties so that his major concerns of security and invasion were managed successfully.

> An overall judgement based on the line of argument pursued throughout the essay is reached.

The answer is focused throughout on the issue of 'success'. It establishes a set of criteria against which to judge success: Henry's aims and these are analysed and a judgement reached as to the success in each area. The argument is well supported with relevant and detailed knowledge. The issues are evaluated and an overall judgement is reached. As a result the answer would be placed at a high level.

Planning an essay

The best essays are based on careful plans. Read the essay and the comments and try to work out the general points of the plan used to write the essay. Once you have done this, note down the specific examples used to support each general point and, where examples are either weak or lacking, use this book to help you find precise details.

3 Henry VIII and Wolsey

Henry VIII's personality and role in government to 1529

Henry VII died in 1509 and was succeeded by his seventeen-year-old son, Henry VIII.

Perhaps the most frequent comments about Henry concern his appearance, which went from tall and attractive in his younger years to fat and bloated by the end of his reign. He is also remembered for his wide range of interests, including jousting, hunting, falconry, music and theology, as well as his six wives.

Henry and the break from his father

Henry wanted to break from the past and the rule of his father, whose latter years had been characterised by meanness and severity. His accession was greeted with joy by many, including writers such as **Thomas More**.

However, there was not a complete break as he kept some of his father's advisors and maintained some of his policies. Yet there were two clear demonstrations of change:
- Dudley and Empson, who had implemented the harsh financial policies, were arrested and executed.
- Henry married Catherine of Aragon.

With both actions Henry won popularity. Henry's father had kept Catherine a virtual prisoner and refused to return her to Spain after Arthur's death. Henry's marriage to Catherine was therefore seen as chivalrous. It also restored the valuable Spanish alliance and gave Henry an ally for his other major aim of building a reputation as a warrior king.

Henry and war

War was seen as chivalrous and a 'kingly' activity, therefore it is not surprising that Henry wanted to prove himself a warrior. He had been brought up on the tales of the legendary King Arthur and the conquests in France of Henry V and the crowning of his son as King of France. The title 'King of France' was also part of Henry's inheritance and he wanted to claim what he believed was rightly his. This would also demonstrate a further break from his father, who had avoided war.

As a result, the desire for war and glory dominated Henry's early years, although reality made it difficult as France was much stronger. Moreover, his ministers were against war because of the cost and advisors such as Bishop Fox and Archbishop Warham wanted to continue the policies of Henry VII. In 1510 they tricked Henry into renewing the truce with France when he wanted to go to war. There were also difficulties with his allies, Spain and the Holy Roman Empire, who were unreliable.

However, in 1512 Henry finally invaded France, but it achieved nothing. Another expedition followed in 1513 and this focused on the area around Calais. The French avoided a full battle, but Henry took the unimportant town of Therouanne. He then lay siege to Tournai, an internationally known city, and its fall gave Henry the glory he desired. This was reinforced by a victory in a skirmish against the French, known as the Battle of the Spurs, which also became a great propaganda victory as some French nobles were captured.

The campaigns had exhausted England financially and was also overshadowed by victory against the Scots at Flodden. However:
- Henry had achieved his aim of glory
- the French agreed to pay the arrears of the French pension
- Henry kept his conquests
- Henry's sister Mary married the aged Louis XII.

Henry and domestic policy

Henry showed little interest in the day-to-day running of affairs and this helped to bring to prominence **Thomas Wolsey**, who had organised supplies for the 1513 campaign. Wolsey supported Henry's war policy, realising the way to rise to power was to back the King. By 1514 Henry was referring nearly all matters of government to him and by 1515 he was Lord Chancellor and a cardinal.

Henry had also won back the support of the nobility through his aggressive policies. His creation of new nobles won him support and was again in contrast to his father. This was further reinforced by his lavish spending and vibrant court.

Spectrum of significance

Below is a key question on why Henry wanted war and a list of possible points. Use your own knowledge and the information on the opposite page to reach a judgement about the relative importance of these points. Write the numbers on the spectrum below to indicate their relative importance. Having done this, write a brief justification of your placement, explaining why some of the factors are more important than others. The resulting diagram could be the basis of an essay plan.

Assess the reasons why Henry VIII wanted to go to war in the years 1509–13.

1 He wanted to appear different to his father, Henry VII.

2 Henry wanted to appear powerful.

3 Henry had a claim to the French throne.

4 War was seen as a chivalrous activity.

5 Henry had been brought up on the stories of the legendary King Arthur and Henry V.

6 Henry wanted to show he was a warrior.

Least important ←——————————————————————————————→ Most important

Reasons behind your placement:

_____

_____

_____

_____

_____

Develop the detail

Below are a sample exam question and paragraph written in answer to this question. The paragraph contains a limited amount of detail. Annotate the paragraph to add additional detail to the answer.

'The main aim of Henry VIII in the years from 1509 to 1529 was to show that he was different from his father.' How far do you agree?

Henry wanted to break from the past and the rule of his father. He was able to demonstrate this in a number of different policy areas. Henry distanced himself from his father in terms of his father's harsh financial measures. His father had also relied a great deal on 'new men' but Henry restored the traditional alliance with the nobility through his policies. Whereas his father had come close to civil war with them by the end of his reign, Henry VIII was able to win their support. The most important way he did this was through his foreign policy, which was very different from that of his father. In order to achieve this break he had to ignore the advice of some of his father's advisors, who had been keen to uphold the old policy. Not only in this area, but Henry VIII also showed a break with the past through his marriage.

Aims and policies in foreign affairs to 1529

Henry wanted to assert himself and this was seen in the early years through his aggressive policy in France. However, the lack of financial resources meant that this approach could not be sustained and for part of the period to 1529 he had to pursue a more peaceful policy and attempt to achieve his aims through treaties and meetings to establish his reputation as the 'most godliest prince that ever reigned'.

Henry's aims

Henry had a number of foreign policy aims and these included:

- achieving military glory
- asserting his claim to the French throne
- securing the succession through his marriage to Catherine
- securing the dynasty, aided by the marriage of Mary to Louis XII
- achieving his imperial ambitions by uniting England and Scotland
- subduing Scotland and protecting England from invasion.

Early campaigns against France

These campaigns (see page 32) helped Henry to achieve some of his gains, but they came at a huge financial cost. However, it was the ability to raise a second force to defeat the Scots at Flodden that was more impressive.

English policy, 1515–20

Two new young and ambitious monarchs came to the thrones of Spain and France – Charles I of Spain and Francis I of France. They wanted to assert themselves and had greater resources available to them than Henry. England's position was further weakened when Mary, who had been married to Louis XII, married the Duke of Suffolk. This was a loss of face for Henry as it was done without permission and lost him the chance to use her in the European marriage market. Furthermore, the French victory in Italy at Marignano and peace between France, Spain and the Emperor left England isolated and forced to change policy.

The Treaty of London, 1518

Wolsey hijacked a papal initiative to launch a crusade against the Turks and turned it into an international peace treaty, the Treaty of London. Henry appeared to be the pivotal power and it brought him glory as England was at the centre of diplomatic activity. However, the gains were short-lived and the balance of power changed with Charles I becoming Holy Roman Emperor.

The Field of Cloth of Gold, 1520

This meeting continued the peaceful policy. First, Charles visited England in May 1520, and then Henry met Francis near Calais. The meeting, known as the Field of Cloth of Gold, achieved nothing of significance but cost a year's income. This was reinforced as England was at war with France in 1521 and when Henry met Charles again they agreed not to make a separate peace with France.

War with France

England sent an army to France in 1523 to aid Charles, but he soon abandoned Henry as he was more concerned with Italy. The English returned in disarray, with the invasion costing £400,000, a year's income, and England was forced to make peace. The situation changed with the Battle of Pavia in 1525 when Charles captured Francis. Henry saw this as the chance to assert his claim to the French throne and ordered Wolsey to raise funds. However, previous financial demands meant money could not be raised. Moreover, Charles refused to attack France so Henry's plans collapsed.

Diplomatic revolution

The failure to get Charles' support led to England allying with France with the Treaty of the More. The League of Cognac was established to try and reverse Pavia and the alliance with France was reinforced by the Treaty of Westminster and the Treaty of Amiens. England declared war against Spain in 1528, but France soon made peace with Spain and England was invited to talks only at the last minute, suggesting it was still a minor power.

The King's Great Matter

By this time, policy was influenced by Henry's desire to annul his marriage to Catherine (see page 40). Catherine was Charles' aunt and a divorce was made more difficult as it would have required a military victory against him. Moreover, France made peace with Spain so England was now isolated.

! Support or challenge? a

Below is a sample essay question which asks you for a judgement on a statement. Using your knowledge and the information opposite, decide whether these statements support or challenge the statement and tick the appropriate box.

'Henry VIII's foreign policy achieved little in the period 1509–29.' How far do you agree?

Statement	Support	Challenge
The Scots were defeated at the Battle of Flodden		
Henry VIII captured Therouanne and Tournai and defeated the French at the Battle of the Spurs		
The Treaty of London was a diplomatic triumph		
The Field of Cloth of Gold brought little gain and was costly		
The marriage of Mary to Louis XII and then the Duke of Suffolk		
War with France in 1523		
England's alliances with France with the Treaty of the More and Westminster		
The diplomatic attempts to get Henry's marriage to Catherine of Aragon annulled		

i Turning assertion into argument a

Below are a sample exam question and a series of assertions. Read the exam question and then add a justification to each of the assertions to turn it into an argument.

How successful was Henry VIII's foreign policy in the period from 1509 to 1529?

Henry VIII's foreign policy was successful only in the short term:

_____

_____

Henry was able to achieve some glory through his policies:

_____

_____

However, he was unable to achieve either of his main goals:

_____

_____

_____

Wolsey's domestic policy

Thomas Wolsey, the son of an Ipswich butcher, rose to power in the early years of Henry VIII's reign. There were a number of reasons for this:

- Wolsey was hard-working and had talent.
- He recognised opportunities for promotion and supported Henry's aggressive foreign policy.
- He was a flatterer.
- The King was less interested in domestic affairs.
- He had been Henry VII's chaplain and had been sent on diplomatic missions for him.
- He had shown organisational skill in the 1513 expedition to France.

As a result of his rise to power he was to be Chief Minister from 1514 until his fall in 1529. Although some have argued he achieved little in domestic affairs, it is unlikely he would have maintained royal favour for so long if that was the case.

Legal reforms

Wolsey attempted to bring greater justice to the legal system. **Civil law** became more important than **common law** as there were fears that the latter led to unjust verdicts based on technicalities. Wolsey heard large numbers of cases, and used the system for his own benefit against those with whom he had a grudge. He used the system to attack the nobility and gentry who, because of his background, treated him with contempt. However, he also ensured that courts dispensed cheap and impartial justice, and were available to the poor who could not afford high fees. The Star Chamber was used to hear cases against the powerful and the Court of Chancery was set up to hear cases brought by the poor. The number of cases was such that the courts could not cope.

Financial reforms

Wolsey introduced the subsidy, which became the standard parliamentary tax, replacing the old fifteenth and tenth. This greatly increased the amount of money brought in and was based on a more realistic assessment of wealth. However, he was still not able to raise enough for Henry's foreign policy. In 1523 he had hoped to raise £800,000, but managed only £300,000. Wolsey then tried to raise funds through the non-parliamentary **Amicable Grant**, which led to massive unrest in East Anglia. Henry had to intervene, cancel the grant and force Wolsey to apologise. Wolsey also tried to increase revenue from crown lands, but that had limited success. Although he raised £820,000 through taxes, by 1520 it did not meet the £1.7 million spent on war.

Social reform

Some historians, because of his legal and social reforms, have argued Wolsey was a champion of the poor. Wolsey attacked the practice of **enclosure**, establishing an enquiry in 1517, with legal action taken against 264 landowners between 1518 and 1529 – 222 were brought to court and verdicts reached on 188. However, this had only a limited impact as in 1523 Wolsey accepted all existing enclosures in return for the parliamentary subsidy. Moreover, many of his actions were against the nobility and gentry, so might have been part of a vendetta against them.

Administrative reform

Wolsey scarcely summoned parliament, calling it only twice in 1515 and 1523, when funds were needed for war. However, some have argued it was because he disliked it and others because his relationship with parliament was poor.

Wolsey was also concerned about the Privy Chamber and in 1526 introduced the Eltham Ordinances. These aimed to improve the finances and efficiency of the chamber. However, the main purpose may have been to control access to the King and increase Wolsey's influence. This would have been important as it followed the failure of the Amicable Grant, at a time when he was being criticised.

! Delete as applicable   a

Below are a sample exam question and a paragraph written in answer to this question. Read the paragraph and decide which of the possible options (in bold) is most appropriate. Delete the least appropriate options and complete the paragraph by justifying your selection.

How successful were Wolsey's domestic policies?

Wolsey's domestic policies were successful to a **great/fair/limited extent**. The changes made to the legal system brought about **very great/great/limited** benefits for the poorer members of society as justice was **more available/less available** to them. The number of cases dealt with by courts **increased/remained the same/declined**. Wolsey's financial policy was also **very successful/mostly successful/a failure** as the amount of money he raised for the King **increased/remained the same/decreased**. His greatest **success/failure** was the introduction of the subsidy, but his attempts to raise money in the 1520s to finance war against France were **more successful/less successful**. Wolsey's social policies were **popular/unpopular** with the nobility who **liked/disliked** his attack on enclosure; however, Wolsey **pushed ahead/abandoned** this policy. Throughout the period Wolsey's relationship with the nobility was **very successful/mostly successful/a failure,** in part this might have been because of his background but also because many of his policies **were supportive of/attacked/exploited** them.

_____

_____

! Complete the paragraph   a

Below are a sample question and a paragraph written in answer to this question. The paragraph contains a point and examples, but lacks a concluding explanatory link back to the question. Complete the paragraph adding this link.

'Wolsey's greatest domestic success was the large amount of money he was able to raise for Henry.' How far do you agree?

Wolsey was able to increase the amount of money that he brought in to fund Henry's ambitious and expensive foreign policy. An important development was the introduction of the subsidy, which became the standard parliamentary tax and replaced the old fifteenth and tenth. The government now had a system that was based on the realistic assessment of wealth. This resulted in a considerable increase in the amount of wealth generated, but in the 1520s was still not enough to fund an invasion of France and forced Wolsey to resort to a non-parliamentary tax, the Amicable Grant, which caused unrest in East Anglia. Another major consequence was that this failure reduced Henry's confidence in Wolsey and may have encouraged further noble opposition towards him as they saw his position was less secure. Wolsey raised in excess of £800,000 for Henry but it did not cover the £1.7 million that was spent on war.

_____

_____

The Church and its condition under Wolsey

Although not Archbishop of Canterbury, Wolsey, as **legatus a latere**, held the highest position in the English Church. Many have argued that he used the position to promote himself and his family. He appeared to personify everything that was wrong with the Church as a **pluralist** and absentee. Although not a monk, he was abbot of the richest abbey, St Albans, and despite his vow of celibacy he fathered children. However, in the 1520s he did carry out some reform, dissolving twenty small monasteries and attempting to start educational reform.

There had also been issues over the Church in the 1510s with the notorious **Hunne Case** and also the **Standish affair**, but in many ways these were exceptions.

Historians have been divided over the condition of the English Church, with some arguing it needed significant reform as it was corrupt and that anti-clericalism was strong, while others have argued it was flourishing.

Arguments that the English Church had support

- There is little evidence the Pope was unpopular, unlike in Germany.
- Clergy at the local level were respected.
- There is little evidence of clerical misconduct.
- Ordination rates remained high, suggesting ordinary people were willing to become clergy.
- Only in the south-east was there evidence of disquiet over paying tithes.
- The Church calendar supported rural activities, with festivals and Church ales.
- **Visitation** evidence found few priests were ignorant.
- Large amounts of literature were bought in urban areas, most notably the Primer, a collection of devotional works, which went through 37 editions between 1510 and 1520 and 41 editions between 1521 and 1530.
- Large-scale building projects continued, with Louth parishioners in Lincolnshire raising £305 to build a new steeple.
- Most still left money in their wills to the Church, which was vital as money was needed to purchase equipment for the celebration of mass.
- The founding of chantries to pray for the souls of the dead continued.
- Parishioners contributed towards the purchase of images.
- There was continued support for religious guilds, with 57 per cent of people in Devon and Cornwall who made wills leaving money to them between 1520 and 1529.

Concerns about the Church

Despite support for the Church it does not mean that there were not concerns. These were particularly noticeable in the south-east and London, with some complaints coming from within the Church itself. In 1511 the Dean of St Paul's, John Colet, preached a sermon attacking abuses, accusing the clergy of being greedy and ambitious. There were bishops who were absent, with Wolsey, for example, not visiting York until 1529. However, many of those absent were on state business and **suffragans** carried out the work. **Pluralism** was common, as seen in the case of Thomas Magnus, who was Archdeacon of the East Riding of Yorkshire, canon at Windsor and Lincoln, Master of St Leonard's Hospital York, Master of the College of St Sepulchre and Sibthorpe College, vicar of Kendal and rector of Bedale, Sessay and Kirby.

Despite these issues, there was not the disquiet with the Church seen in Germany. Support for heretical movements, such as Lollardy, was small, suggesting there is little evidence the Church was under attack. Disputes were not common and most people attended church.

Simple essay style

Below is a sample exam answer. Use your own knowledge and information on the opposite page to produce a plan for this question. Choose four general points, and provide three pieces of specific information to support each general point. The introduction should list the points to be discussed in the essay. The conclusion should summarise the key points and reach a judgement.

To what extent was the Church in England in need of reform in the 1520s?

ⓘ Introducing an argument a

Below are a sample exam question, a list of points to be made in the essay, and a simple introduction and conclusion for the essay. Read the question, the key points, and the introduction and conclusion. Rewrite the introduction and conclusion in order to develop an argument.

How much popular support was there for the Church in England on the eve of the Reformation?

Key points:

- Church ales
- The payment of tithes
- Ordination rates
- Church building projects
- Complaints against the clergy
- The founding of chantries and support for guilds
- Religious literature
- John Colet's sermon

Introduction:

There was evidence of support for the Church on the eve of the Reformation, but there was also some evidence of disquiet. Some people gave money to the Church to help with buildings, while others gave money to found chantries. However, there were some people who made complaints against the clergy, while others refused to pay tithes.

Conclusion:

The Church had support on the eve of the Reformation, with people still giving for its upkeep or others joining as clergy or at least attending church festivals, suggesting that they still supported it. However, there was also dissatisfaction, with complaints from both within and outside the Church, suggesting that not everything was satisfactory.

The divorce and Wolsey's fall

Henry married Catherine of Aragon in 1509. That he began to question the validity of the marriage in the 1520s suggests he was looking for excuses to end it. Henry's desire for a divorce dominated English politics from 1527 to 1533. There were a number of reasons why Henry wanted a divorce:

- Henry believed the marriage was against God's will, believing that the Pope did not have the power to issue the papal dispensation that had allowed him to marry his dead brother's wife. Some have seen this an excuse, but Henry was very religious and had been awarded the title 'Defender of the Faith' following his attack on Luther. He believed that his views were supported by the fact the marriage had not produced a male heir.
- Henry wanted a legitimate heir to secure the dynasty. If his marriage to Catherine was illegitimate it meant their daughter, Mary Tudor, was illegitimate. This could cause unrest when he died. Catherine's last pregnancy had been in 1518 and she was now over 40 so unlikely to conceive. He was concerned as he had made his illegitimate son, Henry Fitzroy, Duke of Richmond and sent him to run the Council of the North, suggesting he might make him successor.
- Henry was in love with **Anne Boleyn**, as shown in the letters he sent her. Anne refused to become his mistress until she was certain to be Queen.

Why did attempts to obtain a divorce fail?

Wolsey assured Henry obtaining a divorce would be easy as he would persuade the Pope the original dispensation was invalid. However, the foreign policy situation complicated matters (see page 34) as Charles, Catherine's nephew, had taken Rome in 1527 and held the Pope virtual prisoner.

Attempts to persuade the Pope that the original dispensation was invalid failed as it would have meant agreeing that the previous Pope had made an error. Henry then tried to argue there was an error in the original dispensation, but Catherine's advisors found a version which satisfied the objections. The third approach was to hear the case in England. Wolsey hoped he would therefore be able to decide the case, but a compromise followed whereby Wolsey was joined by Cardinal Campeggio. Campeggio refused to hurry and when he finally arrived had no intention of reaching a verdict, suspending the court in July 1529.

Wolsey's fall from power

It is difficult to argue against the view that his failure to obtain the divorce was the main reason for Wolsey's fall from power. He had resisted attacks on his position for fifteen years, but this issue was so important to Henry that he could not accept failure. Wolsey had promised it would be easy to obtain and, despite the foreign situation being out of his control, he was still seen as responsible.

The Boleyn **faction** also put pressure on Henry, arguing that Wolsey was being deliberately slow and they claimed that this was because he was hostile to them. There was possibly some truth in this accusation as Anne was more involved in politics than Catherine and might therefore influence Henry. Wolsey might have hoped that delays would cool Henry's infatuation with Anne. However, once it was clear that was not the case, Wolsey's best interest was to obtain a divorce and please the King.

By 1529 Henry was desperate as Anne would not become his mistress and he urgently needed a male heir. The failure of the hearing in England led to Henry using the charge of **praemunire** against Wolsey. Wolsey's fall was not quick. Following his arrest he was released, but then rearrested and brought to London. However, Wolsey died on the way at Leicester on 29 November 1530 before his scheduled execution.

Identify an argument a

Below are a series of definitions, a sample exam question and two sample conclusions. One of the conclusions achieves a high level because it contains an argument. The other achieves a lower level because it contains only description and assertion. Identify which is which. The mark scheme on page 7 will help you.

- Description: a detailed account.
- Assertion: a statement of fact or an opinion which is not supported by a reason.
- Reason: a statement that explains or justifies something.
- Argument: an assertion justified with a reason.

Assess the reasons why Henry wanted a divorce from Catherine of Aragon.

CONCLUSION 1

Henry had married Catherine of Aragon in 1509, but did not start to question the validity of their marriage until the 1520s. Catherine's last pregnancy had been in 1518 and it was unlikely that she would be able to produce any more children as she was now over 40. The only surviving child from the marriage was their daughter, Mary Tudor. Henry had made his illegitimate son, Henry Fitzroy, Duke of Richmond and sent him to run the Council of the North. It appeared as if Henry was preparing to make him his successor. Henry believed that his failure to produce a son from his marriage to Catherine was evidence that the marriage was not legitimate and he was therefore concerned that his daughter, Mary, was therefore not legitimate.

CONCLUSION 2

Henry VIII wanted a divorce from Catherine for a number of reasons; not only had he fallen desperately in love with Anne Boleyn, who refused to become his mistress, but he was concerned about the succession to the English throne. Henry wanted a legitimate son to secure the Tudor dynasty and as Catherine's last pregnancy had been in 1518 and she was now over 40 it was very unlikely that she would produce another child. The matter was complicated further by the fact that Henry believed the reason his marriage had not produced a son was because it was not valid, and that the Pope who had given him the dispensation to marry Catherine did not have the power; this therefore meant that Mary Tudor, the only surviving child from the marriage, was not legitimate, meaning that there was no Tudor to succeed Henry.

Develop the detail a

Below are a sample exam answer and a paragraph written in answer to this question. The paragraph contains a limited amount of detail. Annotate the paragraph to add additional detail to the answer.

'Wolsey's failure to obtain a divorce was the most important reason for his fall from power.' How far do you agree?

Wolsey had resisted attacks on his position for many years over a number of issues and had been able to withstand criticism from groups who disliked him, at least in part because of his background. This would suggest that the failure to gain Henry a divorce was the most important reason. Wolsey also faced factional opposition and they blamed him for being deliberately slow. There may have been some truth in this, and they put pressure on the King to abandon Wolsey. The situation for Wolsey had become very difficult by 1529 and the King was no longer willing to wait for his chief minister to achieve the divorce.

Exam focus

Below are an exam-style essay question and a model answer. Read them and the comments around the answer.

Assess the reasons for Wolsey's fall from power.

Although Wolsey lost favour with Henry following his failure to secure the Amicable Grant and was unpopular with much of the nobility because of both his background and his attempts to restrict their influence, it was his failure to secure the annulment of Henry's marriage from Catherine of Aragon that was the most important reason for his fall from power. This view is reinforced by the fact that he had been able to resist earlier attacks on his power and influence for some fifteen years, but fell from power when he was unable to give Henry what he most wanted.

It is difficult to argue against the claim that Wolsey's failure to obtain a divorce for Henry was the most important reason for his fall. The divorce issue had been Henry's main concern for the previous two years and Wolsey had promised the King that the matter would be easily resolved because of his influence with the papacy. Although many of the issues, such as the foreign situation following the sack of Rome in 1527, meant that the issue was out of Wolsey's control, it did not mean that Henry viewed it that way. By 1529 he was desperate for a divorce as Anne had refused to be his mistress. Every year that passed meant he was unlikely to leave a male heir old enough to rule directly, thereby throwing the country into the dangers of minority rule. The suspension of the papal court that had been set up in England was the trigger for Wolsey's fall. This is clearly evident from the praemunire charges that soon followed against him. However, this failure did not lead to an immediate fall as following his arrest he was released and allowed to reside in modest comfort away from court before being arrested at York. The timing of this event is therefore clear evidence of the importance of his failure to obtain the divorce as a factor in his fall, as he never recovered his influence after the failure of the legatine court at Blackfriars.

Although it was the failure to obtain Henry's divorce that was the most important factor, there is evidence to suggest that the King was influenced by the Boleyn faction in his decision to remove Wolsey. The Boleyns claimed that Wolsey was hostile to them, did not want the divorce and therefore deliberately slowed down the process. If Henry had been initially unwilling to believe this claim, the failure to obtain a verdict from the legatine court in England appeared to confirm to Henry their view was correct. Although faction was not the immediate cause of Wolsey's fall, Anne was much more involved in politics than Catherine and the family was therefore aware that Wolsey had little to gain personally from the divorce as he would lose influence. Such was Anne's hold over Henry, the family was able to exploit Henry's concerns over delays and at least confirm and encourage his decision to remove Wolsey. However, Wolsey was aware of their influence and, if he had tried to delay proceedings in the hope that Henry's infatuation with Anne would end, he would have realised that this had not happened and this may explain why he attempted to speed up proceedings towards the end. Therefore, not only did their influence have an impact on the divorce proceedings, but it encouraged Henry to abandon Wolsey.

The response is aware of a range of issues that need to be discussed, but offers a clear view as to the most important factor.

The factor is clearly explained, narrative about the events is avoided, and an argument as to why it was the most important factor is built up, with details to support the argument.

The role of another factor is discussed and explained, but it is not simply a list of factors. The answer assesses its relative importance and links it to the previous factor.

Wolsey also lacked support from others at court and this made his position more vulnerable. Under pressure from Henry and the Boleyns for the divorce, he would have benefited from support from members of the nobility who had access to Henry. Instead they were able to use the divorce question to exact revenge on a minister they had often despised. Although their lack of support was not a cause of his fall, they did little to attempt to stop it. Wolsey's rise to power in spite of his humble background had antagonised them and this had been made worse by many of his policies and ostentatious display in the building of Hampton Court. Wolsey had alienated the nobility through his social reforms, particularly his attack on enclosures, through which they had benefited, his judicial reforms, and because of his constant determination to prosecute members of the nobility for breaches of the laws against maintenance and affrays. However, even if the nobility resented his influence, most were careful not to go against him as he had a virtual monopoly over patronage and was a magnet for those seeking rewards. It is therefore more valid to suggest that while he had influence they usually worked with him, as it was in their interests, but when he began to lose influence they were quick to desert him, weakening his position further as they had little reason to show loyalty to him; helping his fall from power rather than bringing it about.

> There is a balanced discussion of the role of the nobility in Wolsey's fall. There is detailed knowledge about his relationship with them. The response reaches a balanced judgement as to the role they played in his fall.

Although the divorce was the most important reason for Wolsey's fall, his failure over the Amicable Grant in 1525 might have led Henry to question the judgement and ability of his minister. Wolsey failed to raise sufficient funds for Henry's other main aim – war against France – and in trying to raise funds engineered unrest in East Anglia and opposition from members of the nobility. However, despite failing to raise the sums Henry wanted to take advantage of Francis I's defeat at Pavia and claim the French throne, Wolsey survived. This further suggests that the failure to obtain the divorce was the most important factor as he survived this, but when the chief minister was unable to deliver on something of even greater importance he was removed from office; further evidence of just how important the divorce was to Henry.

> As with the previous paragraph, the factor is analysed and its role compared with the divorce before a judgement is reached.

The divorce was the most important reason for Wolsey's fall. He survived for fifteen years as Chief Minister despite failings, such as the Amicable Grant. However, when he failed to deliver on the issue that mattered the most to Henry he was removed from office fairly quickly. Although the King may have been encouraged by the Boleyn faction and Wolsey, because of his background and policies towards the nobility, lacked support at court, it was ultimately Henry's decision and the Great Matter was so important that Wolsey could not survive.

> The conclusion follows the line of argument outlined in the opening paragraph. There is some knowledge to support the overall judgement.

The answer considers a good range of issues, all of which are analysed and evaluated with consistent focus on the question. Links are made between factors and the argument is supported by detailed and accurate knowledge, which is relevant to the question. Throughout the response a series of interim judgements about the importance of the factor under consideration are made before an overall judgement, which follows logically, is reached. The answer would therefore be placed in a high level.

Reaching the highest level

Using the comments and the mark scheme on page 7, make a list of additional features, both in terms of supporting detail but also argument, that would ensure this answer would reach a high level. Remember that even an answer that is awarded full marks is not a perfect answer, but one that is best fit with the level descriptors in the mark scheme.

4 The reign of Henry VIII after 1529

Religious change and opposition in the 1530s and 1540s

The English Reformation has usually been seen as a religious event with England moving from a Catholic to a Protestant country. However, this view has been challenged and the political causes of the Reformation have now been stressed, with the move to Protestantism slow and far from inevitable. The break from Rome was largely political, because of Henry VIII's need for a divorce.

The changes, 1529–36

Much of the legislation in the early part of this period was designed to put pressure on the Church and prevent it from resisting Henry's desire for a divorce, such as praemunire or the Submission of the Clergy. Pressure was also put on the Pope, with the Act in Restraint of Annates (1532), but this had little impact.

In the period 1533–34, parliament passed a number of laws to abolish papal power in England. The most significant were:
- Act in Restraint of Appeals (1533), which prevented Catherine from appealing to Rome to stop the divorce
- Act of Supremacy (1534), which confirmed Henry as Head of the Church in England.

Other Acts stopped payments to Rome, gave the Archbishop of Canterbury power of dispensation and exemption, ended the Pope's role in Church appointments and gave the Crown power to define religious belief. Although these changes were large, the ordinary people would have noticed little change – that would come only with the Dissolution of the Monasteries (see page 46). There were also no changes to religious doctrine or belief in this period.

Religious developments, 1536–39

This period saw an attack on traditional Catholic practices:
- Act of Ten Articles (1536), which rejected four of the seven sacraments of Catholic belief.
- Royal injunctions (1536), which attacked pilgrimages.
- Bishop's Book (1537), which appeared to reduce the importance of mass and purgatory.
- Matthew's Bible (1537), a Protestant version of the Bible.
- Royal injunctions (1538), which ordered an English Bible in parishes, discouraged pilgrimages and ordered the removal of relics.
- Publication of the Great Bible (1538).

These changes suggested a move to Protestantism, but there was also evidence of traditional practices and beliefs being preserved:
- John Lambert was executed for denying **transubstantiation** (1538).
- The Six Articles (1539) confirmed transubstantiation and forbade communion in both kinds.

Thomas Cromwell probably had a considerable influence on the developments.

Religious developments, 1539–43

Throughout his reign Henry upheld the belief in the real presence at the Eucharist and punished those who disagreed. It would appear that in this period, particularly with the fall of Cromwell (see page 48), Henry was influential in directing policy, with the Six Articles and his marriage to the Catholic, Catherine Howard. He also restricted access to the Bible with the 1543 Act for the Advancement of True Religion and published the conservative King's Book (1543).

Religious developments, 1543–47

There were few changes in this period, although the arrangements for the **Regency Council** did give Protestantism an advantage (see page 56).

By the time of Henry's death, England was not Protestant. Not only had there been very few decisive doctrinal changes, but the majority of the population were still Catholic.

Opposition to the religious changes

The greatest challenge to the changes came in 1536 with the Pilgrimage of Grace (see page 46), but there were some individuals who objected to developments, such as Thomas More, John Fisher and some monks and friars. However, as many of the changes had little impact on people, while there was still no guarantee of a permanent move towards Protestantism there was little reason for opposition. There was also the threat of severe penalties, including death, while Cromwell ran a propaganda campaign both in parliament and in the country to ensure support.

Quick quizzes at **www.hoddereducation.co.uk/myrevisionnotes**

Turning assertion into argument · a

Below are a sample exam question and a series of assertions. Read the exam question and then add a justification to each of the assertions to turn it into an argument.

How far was England Protestant by the death of Henry VIII in 1547?

Most of the early changes had little impact on religious beliefs:

_____

_____

There were some doctrinal changes in the 1530s that suggested a move towards Protestantism:

_____

_____

However, given Henry's religious views and his policies in the period from 1539–43, England remained Catholic because:

_____

_____

Develop the detail · a

Below are a sample exam question and a paragraph written in answer to the question. The paragraph contains a limited amount of detail. Annotate the paragraph to add additional detail to the answer.

How important were Henry VIII's personal views in influencing religious developments in England in the period from 1536 to 1547?

Henry's personal views were very important in influencing religious developments. This was particularly true once he had removed his Chief Minister, who had pursued a more Protestant line. Henry was very traditional in many of his religious beliefs and punished those who disagreed with his views. As a result, any moves towards Protestant views over the Eucharist were resisted and an Act was passed in 1539, which upheld Catholic views. The King was also concerned about who should have access to the Bible and introduced legislation on that despite earlier legislation that had made the Bible available in churches. Henry had also refused to support the Bishop's Book, which attacked some Catholic practices, but did back a more conservative publication in 1543. Even his marriage in 1543 suggests that he wanted to uphold traditional beliefs.

The Dissolution of the Monasteries and the Pilgrimage of Grace

The closure of the monasteries took place in two phases. The smaller monasteries, those with an income of under £200 per year, were closed in 1536, while the larger ones were closed between 1539 and 1540.

The condition of the monasteries

In 1535 a census, the Valor Ecclesiasticus, which looked at the wealth of the Church, was carried out. Cromwell also sent out inspectors to look at the conditions and behaviour within the monasteries. The visitations showed that the monasteries were in a poor spiritual condition. This provided Cromwell with the evidence he needed, with the smaller houses described as 'decayed'. Although the same Act of Dissolution that closed the smaller monasteries praised the larger houses, they were all closed within four years. Most of the larger monasteries surrendered voluntarily, but at the same time a Second Act of Dissolution was passed, another Act was also promised which would use the wealth from the Dissolution to establish colleges and new bishoprics, as well as other social benefits. This meant that when MPs voted for the Second Dissolution they thought funds would go to other uses.

Motives for the Dissolution

There are a number of possible motives for the Dissolution. For Henry it is likely to have been the wealth it would bring him, but for Cromwell religious factors may have played a role.

Religious motives

Reports at the time suggested the behaviour of monks was poor, but it appears these were exaggerated to persuade parliament to agree to the Dissolution as many valued the social as well as religious work they did. Monasteries upheld traditional religious beliefs in purgatory and offered prayers for the dead, which Cromwell and other Protestants disapproved of. They had been dissolved in Germany and Scandinavia and had been criticised by writers, such as Erasmus. Monks were also opponents of the changes and were involved in the Pilgrimage of Grace.

Financial motives

Cromwell had promised to make Henry 'the richest man in Christendom'. Finance was a concern for Henry as he had spent the funds left by his father, and with the break from Rome he now feared invasion and needed to prepare for a Catholic crusade against him, using the money from the monasteries to build fortifications along the south coast. This money also meant he did not need to ask parliament for funds, which would be unpopular. The Dissolution gave Henry a lot of land, which could be used to buy off potential opponents to the changes.

Opposition to the Dissolution and the Pilgrimage of Grace

The dissolution of the smaller monasteries, as well as other religious changes in 1536, may have provoked the largest rebellion in Tudor England, the Pilgrimage of Grace. It raised some 40,000 men, which was far greater than the 8,000 Henry could raise, and involved much of northern England in the period from October 1536 to February 1537, when Bigod's Rebellion in Cumberland was suppressed. During this period the rebels took the second city, York, and captured Pontefract Castle, seen as the gateway to the south.

The demands of the rebels

Not only does the timing of the revolt suggest the main cause was religious, but so too do the demands of the rebels and their rebel ballad, the banner of the Five Wounds of Christ they marched under and the Pilgrim oath. The rebel actions of restoring some monasteries also adds weight to it being a religious rising. However, the rebels also had other complaints:

- There had been a poor harvest in 1535 and 1536.
- Enclosure was an issue around York and the Lake District.
- They complained about rents and entry fines.
- They disliked taxation in peacetime, with the 1534 subsidy.
- There were complaints about Cromwell and other advisors.
- There was anger over the exclusion of Mary from the succession.

Henry was forced to negotiate with the rebels and offer compromises, but he was able to go back on his word when rebels, not trusting him, rose again in 1537. This time a royal army was able to crush the rising.

Quick quizzes at **www.hoddereducation.co.uk/myrevisionnotes**

! Support or challenge? a

Below is a sample exam question which asks how far you agree with a specific statement. Below this is a series of general statements which are relevant to the question. Using your own knowledge and the information on the opposite page, decide whether these statements challenge the statement of the question and tick the appropriate box.

'The most important reason for the Dissolution of the Monasteries was religious reasons.' How far do you agree?

Statement	Support	Challenge
The 1535 Valor Ecclesiasticus revealed how wealthy the monasteries were		
Visitations showed that the monasteries were in a poor spiritual condition		
Cromwell had promised to make Henry the richest man in Christendom		
Monks had been leading opponents of the religious changes		
Monasteries had been closed in other Protestant areas, such as Scandinavia		
Monasteries upheld traditional religious beliefs		
Henry gained a lot of land from the Dissolution which he could use as rewards		
Henry needed money to build defences against a possible Catholic crusade		

! Delete as appropriate a

Below are a sample exam question and a paragraph written in answer to the question. Read the paragraph and decide which of the possible options (in bold) is most appropriate. Delete the least appropriate options and complete the paragraph by justifying your selection.

How serious a threat to Henry VIII was the Pilgrimage of Grace?

The size of the Pilgrimage of Grace meant that the rising was a **minor/considerable/ serious** threat to Henry as he was able to raise a **larger/smaller** force than the rebels. The rebels were also able to gain support from a **small/wide** area in the north and were able to take important towns and castles. However, most of the rebels' demands were **political/religious/economic** and this made it a **minor/serious/considerable** threat to the King. Although the rebellion lasted **days/weeks/months** the King was able to **offer compromises to/negotiate with/suppress** the rebels in early 1537.

_____

_____

The rise and fall of Thomas Cromwell

Thomas Cromwell, like Wolsey, had risen from a very humble background. He owed his rise to being the architect of the break with Rome, possibly suggesting to Henry the way to solve his marriage problem. He had also secured the Royal Supremacy for Henry, brought him considerable wealth through the Dissolution of the Monasteries and made the King supreme in his own realm by removing the power of the Pope.

Cromwell had also been able to use this period to promote Protestantism, as there is little doubt that he had, at least, Protestant sympathies and this is reflected in some of the legislation that was passed in the 1530s. However, it was not just on the religious front that Cromwell was active. He carried out many changes in Tudor government, which led historians such as Geoffrey Elton to argue that the 1530s witnessed a 'Tudor revolution in government'. However, such a view is now widely disputed.

In light of these achievements, it appears that Cromwell should have been indispensable to the King. However, it should be remembered that Wolsey had also served the King well and yet still fell from power, although Cromwell did not fail Henry as Wolsey had done over the divorce.

Cromwell's fall from power

Cromwell was arrested and charged with treason in June 1540 and executed the next month.

What were the reasons for his fall?

- One of the charges against Cromwell was **heresy**. Those who brought the charges against him argued that he was plotting to introduce a fully Protestant Church to England. Such a scenario would have worried Henry given his views, but Cromwell was aware of this and it is therefore unlikely this was his plan. However, he was closely associated with reformist beliefs and legislation and this made the accusations believable. Nonetheless, it is more likely that religion was used as an excuse.
- A major issue was more likely to have been the foreign situation. France and the Habsburgs had made peace leaving England isolated, and there were fears of a Catholic crusade after Henry's **excommunication** in 1538. To counter this, Cromwell had persuaded Henry of the need to ally with the German Protestant princes. This alliance was cemented by the marriage of Henry to Anne of Cleves but the marriage was a disaster as Henry found her unattractive. Moreover, the marriage was unnecessary as France and the Habsburgs were soon at war again. However, it was not the marriage that brought about his fall, as soon after the King rewarded Cromwell with the title Earl of Essex, which was unusual for someone without noble connections. It is unlikely this would have happened if Henry intended to remove him.
- Factional politics provides a more likely explanation for his fall. The Catholic faction, led by **Stephen Gardiner** and the Duke of Norfolk, were able to entice Henry with Norfolk's second niece, Catherine Howard. She was portrayed as an attractive and innocent nineteen year old and after the failure of the Cleves marriage this appealed to Henry, who was soon infatuated with her. It is therefore likely that he believed the stories that he was told about his chief minister.

It was as a result of this that they were able to persuade the King to rush through the process of attainder, which resulted in Cromwell's execution. This view is reinforced by the fact the execution took place on the same day as his marriage to Catherine.

Henry soon realised he had been tricked, but factional struggles would dominate the last years of his rule. The King did not replace Cromwell with another Chief Minister and ruled by himself in a period that saw foreign policy dominate again.

Complete the paragraph   **a**

Below are a sample exam question and a paragraph written in answer to this question. The paragraph contains a point and specific examples, but lacks a concluding explanatory link back to the question. Complete the paragraph adding this link in the space provided.

How important was faction in the fall of Thomas Cromwell?

Cromwell was closely associated with reformist beliefs and was probably instrumental in some of the Protestant legislation of the 1530s. This would undoubtedly have brought him into conflict with the conservative faction led by Bishop Stephen Gardiner and the Duke of Norfolk. They were able to entice Henry with Norfolk's niece, Catherine Howard, who appealed to Henry after his disastrous marriage to Anne of Cleves for which Cromwell had been responsible. Henry soon became infatuated with Catherine, who was portrayed as an attractive and innocent nineteen year old.

_____

_____

 ## Eliminate irrelevance   **a**

Below are a sample exam question and a paragraph written in answer to the question. Read the paragraph and identify parts of the paragraph that are not directly relevant to the question. Draw a line through the information that is irrelevant and justify your deletions in the margin.

Assess the reasons for Cromwell's fall from power in 1540.

Cromwell's fall from power in 1540 was the result of many factors. He had served Henry well and been the architect behind the measures that resulted in the break with Rome and had secured the Royal Supremacy, but this was similar to Cardinal Wolsey who achieved a great deal for Henry. Cromwell had probably achieved more for the King than any other royal servant, bringing about what has been described as a revolution in government and making Henry wealthy through the Dissolution. Despite many achievements, he had alienated many among the nobility because of his background. His position was further weakened by factional struggles between the religious reformists, which Cromwell represented, and the more Catholic faction under Norfolk and Gardiner, which emerged triumphant following the disastrous Cleves marriage, which Cromwell had been responsible for organising. Howard was also able to use his attractive niece, Catherine Howard, to woo Henry and persuade him to believe stories he was told about his Chief Minister.

Henry VIII and faction in the 1540s

The period from 1540 to 1547 is often ignored by historians. Following the fall of Cromwell in June 1540, Henry was left in charge of the day-to-day government, which according to most accounts resulted in a downhill slide. Henry is usually seen as becoming more tyrannical as he became older and health problems dominated. This has led some to argue that he lost control of government and factional struggles dominated, which resulted in government becoming slow or chaotic. However, others have argued that Henry was not manipulated by faction and retained control, using the struggles to strengthen his position. It was only when illness took over that others were able to dominate.

There are a number of events which can be examined in order to determine the validity of the interpretations.

Henry's marriage to Catherine Howard

The last section (page 48) suggested that Henry was manipulated by faction to marry Catherine and remove Thomas Cromwell, supporting the view that he had lost control of government.

The fall of Catherine Howard

Catherine fell from power quickly as she soon became bored with the ageing King and was unable to pretend she loved him. Opponents of Norfolk and Gardiner seized their chance. **Thomas Cranmer** told Henry of her adultery and pre-marital affairs, but was so scared of his reaction that it was done via letter. Henry did not want to believe it, but confessions forced him to accept the truth. Although Catherine was executed, Henry was not tyrannical and allowed Norfolk to withdraw from court, recognising his previous loyal service. His choice of Catherine Parr as his final wife also suggests he had become more realistic.

Attacks on Thomas Cranmer

The fall of Cromwell left Cranmer, Archbishop of Canterbury and the man who had granted the annulment of Henry's marriage to Catherine of Aragon, vulnerable to attack from the Catholic faction. They accused him of being a heretic and wanted him arrested.

Henry warned Cranmer of the plot, gave him a ring as a sign of confidence and finally ordered Cranmer to investigate the charges himself. As a result, they were dropped. Henry had stood by a loyal servant, suggesting he was in control. However, it could be argued that the King could have stopped the case developing and avoided the fears Cranmer must have had when he was arrested, suggesting Henry wanted to show his power and how everyone depended upon him.

The arrest of Catherine Parr

The arrest of Catherine does suggest Henry enjoyed court intrigue. The Catholic faction, having failed with Cranmer, now attacked the Queen. She sympathised with reformist beliefs and they gave Henry evidence she was a heretic. Henry allowed her accusers to confront her with evidence of heresy. It appears she was told of the charges as she was allowed to see her husband, but it must have been frightening. She was able to convince her husband and agreed to follow his views and therefore when the opponents arrived to arrest her they were greeted with abuse from Henry. This was further evidence that the King was in control.

The fall of Gardiner and Norfolk

The fall of Gardiner and Norfolk, as well as the Earl of Surrey, suggests that, despite Henry's effort to maintain a balance between rival factions, the reformists triumphed in his final year. A trumped-up charge brought about Gardiner's fall, further suggesting the reformists' dominance. The fall of Norfolk's son, Surrey, reinforces this. He was executed for putting part of the royal coat of arms on his emblem without permission. Norfolk was arrested and imprisoned in the Tower, and would have been executed if Henry had not died.

The removal of Gardiner and Norfolk supports the view that by the end of his reign Henry had lost control.

! Spider diagram

Use the information on the opposite page and page 48 to add detail to the spider diagram on factional conflicts below.

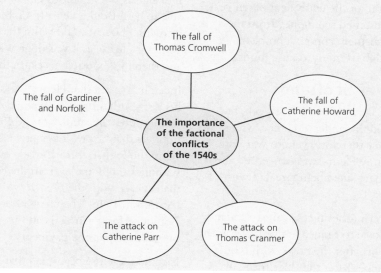

! You're the examiner　a

Below are a sample exam question and a paragraph written in answer to the question. Read the paragraph and the mark scheme provided on page 7. Decide which level you would award the paragraph. Write the level below, along with a justification for your decision.

'Henry VIII was always able to manage the factional conflicts of the 1540s.' How far do you agree?

Henry was certainly able to manage the attempts by the Catholic faction to bring down his Archbishop, Thomas Cranmer, and his wife, Catherine Parr. In both instances he stood by a loyal servant and his wife, suggesting that he was in control. Not only that, but in the Cranmer case he could have stopped the incident from developing and avoided the fear that Cranmer must have felt when he was arrested, suggesting that Henry wanted to demonstrate his power. Similarly, in the Catherine Parr case, she was forced to submit to his views and when opponents arrived to arrest her they were subject to abuse from the King, further evidence of Henry controlling the situation. However, in the last year of his life he was less in control as the reformist faction were able to secure the removal of Gardiner over a trumped-up charge and bring about the removal of Norfolk's son, Surrey, while also having Norfolk arrested. Although Henry had therefore been able to control factional conflict in the early 1540s, he had lost control by the last year of his life and the reformist factions were able to triumph.

Level:

Reason for choosing this level and this mark:

_____

_____

Henry VIII's foreign policy in the 1540s

Foreign policy and war against France and Scotland dominated Henry's last years. It has been seen as a costly failure as some £2 million, or the equivalent of ten years' income, was spent. It consumed the money from the Dissolution and created further economic problems because of the need for **debasement** to raise funds.

Henry's aims over Scotland

Henry arranged to meet James V in 1541 at York, but James failed to appear and this angered Henry, who saw it as a personal insult. Henry therefore went to war with Scotland in 1542. Certainly Henry was concerned about prestige and would not have liked being treated with contempt.

Henry also had longer-term grievances against Scotland:
- James had remained loyal to France in the 1530s when England needed support after the break with Rome.
- James had protected rebels after the Pilgrimage of Grace.
- The Scots had undertaken border raids after England signed an Anglo-Imperial alliance in 1542.

It was in response to these raids that an English army had been sent north and defeated the Scots at Solway Moss in November 1542. This had important consequences as James V died soon after, with the result the new ruler was a baby, Mary. This meant Scotland was weak and Henry saw the chance to settle the border problem by marrying his son, Edward, to Mary. The marriage was agreed by the Treaty of Greenwich in 1543, but the Scots soon rejected the agreement. As a result, a series of raids were launched by the English in 1544 and 1545, but this policy of 'rough wooing' failed and Mary was later married to the French Dauphin. The English were unable to inflict a major defeat on the Scots who were therefore able to continue their raids. The English attacks also brought the French and Scots even closer together, culminating in the marriage of Mary and the Dauphin.

Henry's aims with France

During his wars against France (1542–46) Henry was able to gain Boulogne in 1544, but the financial cost was immense. Henry could claim that it showed England was a military force, as it was done without the help of allies and therefore boosted his claim to glory.

It can be argued that Henry was simply looking to regain his lost youth, or that he wanted to regain his standing in Europe after the failures of the 1520s (see page 34). It is unlikely that he saw it as a prelude to a further attempt to claim the French throne, made even less likely by the withdrawal of Charles from the conflict. Henry soon made peace with the French with the Treaty of Camp (Ardres) in 1546. The terms allowed England to keep Boulogne for seven years and France agreed to pay the outstanding pension payments.

It could therefore be argued that his policy against France was more successful than that against Scotland.

Assessment of Henry's foreign policy in the 1540s

- The demands of war had resulted in debasement, heavy taxation, forced loans and borrowing on the Antwerp money market.
- Henry was without allies as the Habsburgs made peace with France.
- France was now free to attack England and the Auld Alliance with Scotland had been strengthened.
- The French fleet was able to attack the Isle of Wight.

It must therefore be decided whether:
- Henry failed to achieve success and wasted a large amount of money trying to gain military glory
- Henry maintained England's position in Europe, secured the northern border by defeating the Scots and improved England's hold over Calais by capturing Boulogne.

Simple essay style

Below is a sample exam question. Use your knowledge and information on the opposite page to produce a plan for this question. Choose four general points and provide three pieces of specific information to support each general point. Once you have planned your essay, write the introduction and conclusion for the essay. The introduction should list the points to be discussed in the essay. The conclusion should summarise the key points and justify which point was the most important.

Assess the reasons why Henry VIII went to war with France and Scotland in the 1540s.

RAG – Rate the timeline

Below are a sample exam question and a timeline. Read the question, study the timeline and, using three coloured pens, put a Red, Amber or Green star next to the events to show the following:

- Red: events and policies that have no relevance to the question.
- Amber: events and policies that have some significance to the question.
- Green: events and policies that are directly relevant to the question.

How successful was Henry VIII's foreign policy in the 1540s?

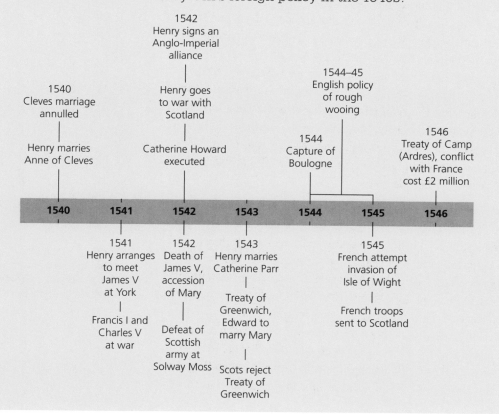

Exam focus

Below are an exam-style essay question and model answer. Read them and the comments around the answer.

How Protestant was England by the death of Henry VIII in 1547?

England was not Protestant by the death of Henry VIII. Although there had been some legal changes that had attacked Catholic beliefs and practices in the late 1530s, many had been reversed in the 1540s. Moreover, the large majority of the population were still Catholic in their beliefs as is shown by evidence from wills, with only a few in the south-east and East Anglia having adopted reformist beliefs. The position was further reinforced by the views of Henry VIII who did not have Protestant leanings even though he had broken from Rome in 1534. However, the introduction of the Great Bible and the nature of the Regency Council that Henry left for his son, Edward, did mean that there was the potential for Protestantism to take root, but it would be a slow process.

> A clear view is offered in the opening sentence.

> The issues to be discussed are raised and briefly explained.

> There is balance to the argument and the opening sentence is qualified.

The changes that were introduced during the Henrician reformation were mostly legal, not doctrinal, meaning that England remained a Catholic nation, albeit without the Pope as the Head of the Church. All of the changes up until 1536 had been legal in nature, which meant that, even if Henry had desired to establish a Protestant church, he would have had only ten years in which to achieve it. However, it is certainly true that there appeared to be some moves towards Protestantism in the 1530s; the most notable being the Dissolution of the Monasteries, which attacked the belief in purgatory as many monks spent significant amounts of time praying for the souls of the dead. There were also attacks on some Catholic practices, such as pilgrimages, with the 1536 Injunctions, and Catholic traditions, such as relics, with the 1538 Injunctions. The 1536 Act of Ten Articles had also rejected four of the seven sacraments of Catholic belief. Perhaps most importantly, an English Bible had been introduced in 1539 which gave the laity access to the scriptures and allowed them, rather than just the priest, to interpret it. Despite these developments, the changes made in the period from 1539 to the end of Henry's reign suggest that England was still officially Catholic, with the 1539 Act of Six Articles reversing many of the changes, while the Act for the True Advancement of Religion of 1543 restricted access to the Bible and therefore limited development of Protestant thought. Although the production of an English Litany in 1544, which replaced the Catholic use of a Latin Litany, might suggest that moves towards Protestantism were still occurring, this was not the case as priests did not have to use the new version. Therefore, although some religious legislation did bring about changes in doctrine, much of it was reversed in the 1540s, leaving England still a Catholic country in terms of doctrine.

> There is clear focus on the question, with good supporting detail to sustain a consistent argument, which is linked back to the question in the last sentence.

Henry's own personal beliefs also ensured that England was still a Catholic country. The central Catholic doctrine of transubstantiation was still upheld and Henry ensured that this was enforced, with John Lambert executed in 1538 for rejecting it, and the Act of Six Articles confirming it and forbidding the Protestant practice of taking communion in both kinds. Therefore, although Thomas Cromwell had taken England down a more reformed route in the 1530s, his fall in 1540 and Henry's own beliefs ensured that England would remain largely Catholic in doctrine. Henry's decision not to replace Cromwell with another Chief Minister ensured that decisions remained firmly in the King's hands until his declining health allowed the potential for a move towards a more reformed religion with the appointments to the Regency Council and the appointment of the Protestant John Cheke as tutor to the young Edward. Although

> The paragraph discusses a further issue raised in the opening and again discusses it in a balanced manner and the view is supported with evidence.

Quick quizzes at **www.hoddereducation.co.uk/myrevisionnotes**

these developments gave Protestantism the potential to triumph, little had been achieved by 1547, and the ease with which Mary would be able to restore Catholicism in 1553 is further evidence that Catholic belief was still firmly rooted in England even after the rule of Edward VI.

If there was little evidence from the centre that England was Protestant, it is unlikely that there would be large-scale conversion in the countryside and this view is supported by the numerous local county studies. Evidence from wills in counties, such as Gloucestershire, show that most were still Catholic in their wording, making reference to the Virgin Mary and putting their trust in salvation through Christ's death, rather than the Protestant belief that they were assured of salvation. There is some evidence of limited moves towards Protestantism in areas such as London and Kent, but even in London the numbers were only 20 per cent, and further north and west there were even fewer. However, even if there is little evidence of conversion to Protestantism, there is evidence to suggest that the attacks by the government on traditional practices had had some impact as the numbers coming forward for ordination had declined and the amount of money left for church building had also fallen. Therefore, even if England was not Protestant, confidence in the Church had declined and would be difficult to restore.

> The debate is widened from the centre and government to beliefs in the localities and again precise evidence is used to support the argument. Once again the discussion is balanced and a judgement is reached.

Although England was not Protestant by the death of Henry VIII, traditional Catholic practices had been attacked and the translation of the Bible into English did have a lasting impact, ensuring religious belief would not be the same again. The difficulties Edward's government faced in imposing Protestantism and the ease with which Mary was able to restore Catholicism further support the view that there was only a small minority who were Protestant in 1547. Most of the changes had been to England's relationship with Rome, while doctrinal changes had been limited and had had little impact on ordinary people. Henry himself continued to uphold many Catholic practices, supporting transubstantiation and leaving money for masses to be said for his soul. It would not be until much later in Elizabeth I's reign that England could be called Protestant.

> An overall judgement based on the earlier paragraphs is reached and knowledge from outside the dates in the question is used to further support the overall argument. The judgement reflects the line of argument pursued in the main body of the essay.

This is a strong answer which shows a good understanding of the demands of the question, considering both the official position of Protestantism and people's beliefs. The answer is focused on 1547 throughout and the knowledge used is both precise and relevant. There are interim judgements reached at the end of each paragraph in relation to the issue discussed before the overall judgement pulls them together. The answer would be placed in a high band.

Characteristics of an A-grade essay

You have now considered four sample high-level essays. Use these essays to make a bullet-pointed list of the characteristics of an A-grade Period Study essay. Use this list when planning and writing your own practice exam essays.

5 The stability of the monarchy

The problem of Edward VI's age

REVISED

In 1543 Henry VIII had issued a Third Succession Act which confirmed that if **Edward** died without heirs the throne would pass to Mary Tudor; 'and should the Lady Mary die without heirs, then the crown shall pass to the Lady Elizabeth and to her heirs'. This Act reversed the earlier Succession Acts, which excluded both Mary and Elizabeth from the succession, although it did not reverse their illegitimacy.

As Henry's health declined during 1546 he was aware that Edward would come to the throne as a minor. As a result, Henry wanted to try and avoid disputes about the succession and in his will confirmed the terms of the Third Succession Act.

The establishment of the Regency Council

Henry's concern about political stability was seen in his establishment of a Regency Council. This was balanced between 'reformists', led by Seymour (later the **Duke of Somerset**), and the 'Catholics' under Norfolk and Gardiner. However, this was undermined by the actions of **William Paget** and Denny, who left plenty of space in the King's will for changes to the King's wishes to be made and it appears that details about the Council were added only when the King was close to death and unable to prevent them. Moreover, their task was made easier as Gardiner had been removed and Norfolk was in the Tower (see page 50).

The changes did not even require Henry's signature as Denny controlled the dry stamp of the King's signature, which could be inked in. He and Paget were also able to keep Henry's death quiet for a few days so the reformists were able to consolidate their position and Somerset establish himself and exercise virtual royal power.

The problem of a minor on the throne

There had been minors on the throne before:
- Henry III was nine when he came to the throne; civil war broke out but only after he came of age.
- Richard II was ten when he came to the throne in 1377; he was deposed in 1399 but that was because of his rule after he came of age.
- Henry VI was eight months old in 1422 and although his reign witnessed the Wars of the Roses, England was relatively stable during the minority.

- Edward V was twelve when he succeeded Edward IV in 1483. He was imprisoned and probably murdered by his uncle and supposed protector, Richard III, which lost Richard support and aided Henry Tudor in his claim.

There were concerns a minor would create instability because:
- he would be unable to lead troops in battle
- other states might look to exploit the weakness of a minor and attack
- England might return to civil war as had happened in the fifteenth century
- he would be unable to control factional struggles, similar to those of the last years of Henry VIII (see page 50)
- in an age of personal monarchy, there were concerns about his image; it would be difficult to portray Edward as powerful or military adept.

However, the later image of Edward as a sickly child was not true when he came to the throne. There was every expectation in 1547 that he would reach adulthood and produce an heir.

The emergence of Somerset

Somerset's assumption of power was unsurprising as he was Edward's uncle and had built up a reputation as a successful soldier during the campaigns against Scotland in the 1540s. The transfer of power to him was smooth and there were good arguments against a Regency Council of sixteen with every member having an equal voice as it was very unlikely any decisions would be reached. However, some questioned the legality of Somerset's power as it went against Henry's wishes.

Mind map

Make a copy of the mind map below and use the information on the opposite page to show how each issue explains why there were concerns about a minor on the throne.

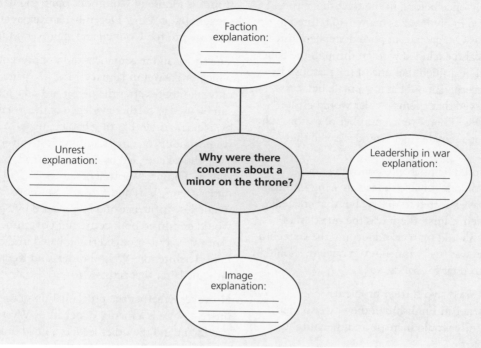

- Faction explanation: _____
- Unrest explanation: _____
- Why were there concerns about a minor on the throne?
- Leadership in war explanation: _____
- Image explanation: _____

Spot the inference

High-level answers avoid just summarising or paraphrasing the sources, and instead make inferences from the sources. Below are a source and a series of statements. Read the source and decide which of the statements:

- make an inference from the source (I)
- paraphrase the source (P)
- summarise the source (S)
- cannot be justified from the source (X).

How useful is the source as evidence of the problems of establishing stability after the death of Henry VIII?

Statement	I	P	S	X
Henry VIII's death caused unrest				
There were concerns among the Council on how to achieve stability				
The late King's will was enforced and Somerset became Lord Protector				
Edward was proclaimed King when his father's death was announced, the Council enforced the King's will and appointed Somerset as Protector				

SOURCE

From Edward VI's chronicle, 1547.

He [in his private diary Edward always referred to himself as 'he'] was suddenly proclaimed King on the day his father's death was announced in London, where there was great lamentation. He spent three weeks in the Tower while the Council enforced the late King's will. They thought best to choose the Duke of Somerset as Lord Protector of the Realm and Governor of the King's person during his minority, being but nine years old. He sat at dinner with the crown on his head and Lords in the hall beneath.

The problem of gender and Mary's marriage

The accession of a female ruler caused serious concerns in sixteenth-century society. England had been ruled by a female ruler only once before, in the twelfth century. That had resulted in civil war as many had refused to accept Matilda as Queen and supported Stephen instead. Some countries also excluded women through the Salic law and it could be argued that one of the reasons Henry VIII was so concerned about having a male heir was because he believed that a female ruler would create dynastic weakness. There were a number of reasons why it was feared that a female ruler would weaken the monarchy:

- A woman would be unable to control faction.
- A woman would be unable to lead an army into battle.
- A woman was expected to marry, but that created further problems. First, there was the question of whom Mary should marry, and second, the sixteenth-century view was that women, even queens, should be subservient to their husbands.

This therefore raised two further problems:

- If Mary married an Englishman the power of her husband's family would increase and they might dominate court.
- If Mary married a foreigner there were fears that the country would be dominated by foreigners.

Mary's marriage

The Scottish theologian John Knox wrote *The First Blast and Trumpet Against the Monstrous Regiment of Women* in which he expressed his view that it was unnatural and insulting to God for a woman to rule. However, it was not that, but rather Mary's decision to marry Philip of Spain that caused the problems. There were only two realistic candidates:

- Edward Courtenay, Earl of Devon, who was backed by Gardiner.
- Philip of Spain, who was backed by Paget.

Courtenay was descended from royal blood, but Mary's preference was Philip as it would bring England closer to the Habsburgs, the family to which her mother, Catherine of Aragon, was related.

Philip might be a powerful ruler who could protect Mary, but as she was expected to be subservient she could be dragged into wars which would not benefit the nation. These fears played a significant role in Wyatt's rebellion (see page 92) of 1554, although it can also be argued that it was Mary's skill that defeated him, showing that female rule was able to preserve the monarchy.

Mary informed the Council on 27 October 1553 that it was her intention to marry Philip. There was a petition from the House of Commons opposing her decision, but she ignored it. On 7 December a marriage treaty was presented to the Council and approved in January 1554.

The treaty and reassurances did not prevent rebellion, which broke out in January 1554 (see page 92). This was only six months after the defeat of **Lady Jane Grey** and can be used as further evidence of the instability caused by a female ruler. Plotting had begun as soon as there were rumours of a marriage and it involved members of the political elite, led by Sir James Croft, Sir Peter Carew and Sir Thomas Wyatt. These men had all held office under Henry VIII and Edward, but now feared they would lose influence and be replaced by Spaniards who would dominate both court and government. The initial plan was a four-pronged rising based in Devon, Leicestershire, the Welsh borders and Kent, but it was only the latter that actually rose.

However, whether the proclamation of the marriage was the real cause is a matter of debate as Wyatt was a Protestant and the other leaders all had links with the reformed faith. The rebels had planned to marry Elizabeth to Courtenay, but he disclosed the scheme and this forced the rebels to act early. Despite this, the situation was serious as a royal force under Norfolk sent to confront the rebels deserted. The rebels did get to the gates of the city of London, but Mary's resolution and refusal to leave the city were factors in its defeat and again a sign that a female ruler was not necessarily weak.

Despite the defeat of the rebellion, it did have an impact on stability as the marriage did not take place until twelve months after Mary came to the throne, and after the marriage Philip spent more time abroad than in the country, limiting his influence to, at best, a distant confidant.

Using the provenance

Sources A and B show different explanations given for Wyatt's rising. Identify the difference and use the provenance to help you decide which might be more reliable.

Difference:

_____

_____

_____

Which might be more reliable?

_____

Why?

_____

_____

_____

SOURCE A

Thomas Wyatt explains the reasons for the rebellion in a proclamation, 25 January 1554.

We write to you as friends, neighbours and Englishmen, concerning Queen Mary's declared intention to marry a foreigner, and request you to join us to prevent this. We swear to you before God that we seek no harm to the Queen, but merely wish her better advice. Our wealth and health depend on it. A hundred armed Spaniards have already arrived at Dover and travelled through Kent on their way to London. We require you to assemble with us as much support as possible, to help us protect liberty and the commonwealth.

SOURCE B

An account written for the government explains the rising.

Wyatt, proceeding in his detestable purpose, armed himself and as many as he could. And, considering that the restoring of the newly-forged religion was not a cause general enough to attract all sorts to support him, he determined to speak no word of religion but to make the colour of his commotion only to withstand strangers and to advance liberty.

AS-level question

Read Source C and answer the following question:

Source C refers to the defeat of Wyatt's rebellion. How useful is it for understanding why Mary Tudor was able to rally support against Wyatt?

SOURCE C

A contemporary records Mary's reaction to Wyatt's march on London.

On 1 February the Queen went to the Guildhall and declared to the audience the wicked plan of the traitor Wyatt, which was utterly to deprive her of her crown, and to ransack the city. She spoke so nobly, with so good spirit, and with so loud a voice, that all the people might hear her Majesty, and were comforted in their hearts with so sweet words which made them weep with joy to hear her Majesty speak. On 3 February the Queen appointed Lord William Howard to be Captain General, with the Lord Mayor for the defence of the city.

The Succession in 1553

In the early months of 1553 Edward VI's health began to deteriorate, and despite treatment, he continued to decline. According to the Succession Acts and Henry's will, the throne was to pass to Edward's half-sister, Mary. However, during the spring and summer a plot developed to change the succession so as to exclude Mary. Most accounts suggest that the scheme was the work of the Lord President of the Council, Northumberland. These accounts argue that he was behind it because:

● it was essential to preserve his power
● as a Protestant he would lose power when the Catholic Mary came to the throne.

These accounts have therefore argued that he arranged the marriage of his son, Guildford Dudley, to Lady Jane Grey in order to achieve it. This was soon followed by Edward changing his will and naming Jane Grey as his heir.

However, there is also evidence to suggest that Edward was the driving force behind the attempts:

● He was playing a greater role in government, attending Privy Council meetings and setting some agendas.
● Edward was a committed Protestant and wanted to stop the throne passing to his Catholic half-sister.
● Edward wanted the religious reform programme he had started to continue.

The Devise

The Devise for the Succession was initially drawn up in May 1553. It named the male heirs of the Grey family as the successors, but there were no male heirs and there was no likelihood of any being born before Edward died, as his health was declining rapidly. Therefore the initial Devise was altered and Jane Grey was made heir. It was only with this change that Northumberland's importance increased as when Guildford married Jane she was not heir.

The plot

The plot was poorly managed and this supports the view that it was Edward, rather than Northumberland, who was behind its organisation:

● As an experienced soldier, Northumberland would have ensured he had sufficient forces to take control, but the professional force had been dismissed in 1552.
● He would have ensured Mary was captured, but she escaped to East Anglia.
● He would have launched a propaganda campaign to prepare the nation for the change in the succession.

When Edward died on 6 July the news was kept quiet for two days. Mary responded quickly and proclaimed herself Queen and sent letters to the Privy Council and important towns informing them, thus behaving as if she considered herself the rightful and legitimate monarch. The question of legitimacy was important for the ruling class, because if they supported an illegal claimant all laws could be challenged and their right to land questioned. It was in their interests to support the rightful ruler.

Although Jane was proclaimed Queen, against her wishes, on 10 July, her rule did not last (see page 90) and the rebellion soon collapsed.

Mary Tudor's death

If the death of Edward VI had created instability with the raising of armed forces, this was not the case in 1558. However, even in 1553, Lady Jane Grey ruled for only nine days and the ruling elite supported the rightful monarch, backing Mary once Northumberland left London.

Mary made no attempt to alter the succession in 1558, although she did try and persuade Elizabeth to maintain the Catholic faith. When she died, the crown was offered peacefully to her sister, suggesting that legitimacy and the succession as stated by Henry in the Third Succession Act was more important than issues of religious belief.

Support or challenge? ⓐ

Below is an exam-style question that asks you to agree with a specific statement, followed by a series of sources relevant to the question. Use your own knowledge and the information on the opposite page to decide whether the sources support or challenge the statement in the question and explain why in the boxes.

Using these three sources in their historical context, assess how far they support the view that Mary's legitimacy was the most important reason people supported her in 1553.

	Support	Challenge
Source A		
Source B		
Source C		

SOURCE A

An anonymous writer explains why people supported Mary. John Foxe later used this as a source for his Acts and Monuments.

After King Edward's death the Council proclaimed Lady Jane as queen. But, partly because of the right of Mary's title and partly because of the malice that the people bore to the Duke of Northumberland for the death of the Duke of Somerset and his other cruelty, the majority of the commons with some nobles sided with Lady Mary, who proclaimed herself queen.

SOURCE B

A writer explains his concerns about the change to the succession. From A Poetical Autobiography of Sir Nicholas Throckmorton, *written before 1571.*

Immediately I heard of King Edward's death. I sorrowfully left Greenwich and went to our family home in London. My brother guessed by my depressed mood that the King was dead and I told them this was so. I revealed to them the cover-up that had taken place and how the Council intended to proclaim Queen Jane. I did not love Catholicism but detested the wicked plan to exclude rightful heirs. I was looking for a solution; there was no need to injure Mary in this way.

SOURCE C

A writer explains why Suffolk men supported Mary. From John Foxe, Acts and Monuments, *written in the mid 1550s.*

The first to resort to her were the Suffolk men who, being always forward in promoting the proceedings of the gospel, promised her their aid provided she would promise them no innovations would be made in religion. She agreed.

Doing reliability well ⓐ

Below are an exam-style question and a set of definitions listing common reasons why sources can be unreliable. Using Sources A–C above, for each source write a critical account of whether it is a reliable or unreliable piece of evidence, justifying your answer by referring to the definitions below.

Using these three sources in their historical context, assess how far they support the view that Mary's legitimacy was the most important reason people supported her in 1553.

- **Vested interest**: the source is written so that the writer can protect his or her own power or interests.
- **Second-hand report**: the writer is not in a position to know and is relying on someone else's information.
- **Expertise**: the source is written on a subject that the author is an expert in.
- **Political bias**: the source is written by a politician and it reflected their political views.
- **Reputation**: the source is written to protect the writer's reputation.

Faction and its impact under Edward VI

The last years of Henry VIII's reign had seen a factional struggle (see page 50), but this appeared to have ended with the triumph of Somerset and the 'reformist faction' over the 'Catholic faction' with the defeat of Henry's plan for a balanced Regency Council. However, although the reformists dominated government, the events of the summer of 1549 gave the Catholic faction an opportunity to reassert itself.

The impact of the 1549 unrest

Although the unrest in the countryside was put down, the ruling elite were concerned by the disorder, particularly as some of the rebels' complaints were against them. Not only that, but there was also disquiet within governing circles about the personal nature of Somerset's government, as letters from Paget, a close advisor of the Protector, reveal. It led to the formation of an anti-Somerset faction.

The anti-Somerset faction

The group that was formed had little in common, except a dislike of Somerset's methods and policies. It included such diverse figures as Paget, Warwick, who was made Duke of Northumberland in 1547, and Wriothesley. The latter was opposed to Somerset's religious policies, Warwick may have seen an opportunity to advance his own power, while Paget was concerned about Somerset ignoring his advice. It was the events of the summer of 1549 that provided this group with the opportunity to act.

Somerset's loss of power

As Somerset's hold on power declined, he retreated to Hampton Court with Edward. On 5 October he summoned loyal subjects there to defend him and the King, but the next day moved to Windsor with Edward. However, Edward fell ill, claimed he was a prisoner and abandoned his uncle. Edward stated that Somerset had threatened riots if he was removed from power. Although Somerset denied this, he could not contradict the King and within a week was removed.

The triumph of Warwick

Although Somerset had been removed, Warwick's triumph was far from guaranteed. The Council contained a majority of religious conservatives who did not trust Warwick. He brought in his own allies so that he had a Protestant majority, but in early December there were rumours of a Catholic plot to remove him. Warwick seized the opportunity, declaring that any who attacked Somerset were attacking him. By January 1550 the leading Catholics the Earls of Arundel and Southampton had been dismissed and Warwick was Lord President of the Council. He placed his own supporters in important positions around Edward, but in order to succeed he had been forced to ally with more religiously radical members and this would have an impact on religious developments (see page 70).

Once he was secure he attempted a reconciliation with Somerset.

Despite the factional struggle lasting from October 1549 until early 1550, the administration of the country continued to function and did not impact on the efficiency of the government. The crisis in October was short-lived and did not threaten the monarchy.

The execution of Somerset

Warwick released Somerset from jail, his goods were restored and his daughter married Warwick's son. He was also restored to court and the Privy Council. However, Somerset continued to plot in an attempt to recover his position and this led the Privy Council to execute him on 22 January 1552, although some of the evidence may have been fabricated to justify his death.

Linking sources

Below are a question and the four sources referred to in the question. In one colour draw links between the sources to show ways in which they show that political instability was caused by the ambition of councillors.

Read Sources A–D. How far do they show that ambition was the main cause of political instability in the period 1549–52?

SOURCE A

William Paget writes to Protector Somerset, July 1549. Paget was one of his advisors.

The King's subjects out of all discipline and all obedience, and care for neither you or the King. What is the cause? Your softness, your wish to be good to the poor. It is a pity that your gentle approach should cause such evil as the rebels now threaten.

SOURCE B

A chronicle outlines the charges against Somerset in October 1549.

First that through his malicious and evil government, the Lord Protector had caused all the recent unrest in the country. Second, he was ambitious and sought his own glory. Third, that he had ignored the advice of his councillors. Fourth, that he had told untruths about the Council to the King.

SOURCE C

A contemporary relates the events leading to Somerset's execution.

Somerset was the head of a conspiracy against the whole Council, and more particularly against the Duke of Northumberland, whom Somerset pursued with a deadly hatred, since Northumberland had been foremost among those who deprived him of the rank of Lord Protector.

SOURCE D

A contemporary explains why the Privy Council executed Somerset.

The whole council decided that they would no longer endure that excessive arrogance of the Duke of Somerset, that made it quite clear that if he were released from imprisonment, he would raise rebellions which would endanger the whole kingdom.

Add your own knowledge

Annotate Sources A–D with your own knowledge to add evidence which either supports or challenges the view presented in each source about whether ambition was the main cause of instability in the period 1549–52.

Faction under Mary

One of the major concerns about a female ruler was that it was believed they would be unable to control factions. This had already appeared to be the case over Mary's proposed marriage, with two of her leading councillors supporting different suitors. There were also fears that a Spanish marriage would create factional strife between English courtiers worried about their positions and patronage and the expected influx of Spanish courtiers, who they believed would dominate the court and be given positions within the administration. Despite these concerns, there is no evidence that it had an impact on the efficiency of the administration.

Divisions within the Privy Council

Mary's Privy Council was large as she brought in her own supporters who had helped her gain the throne, but also kept many experienced administrators. This has led some to argue that it was ineffective. However, this view can be challenged because:

- it was rare for all councillors to be present
- the average size of meetings was similar to those held under Northumberland
- committees were established in 1554 which excluded casual councillors
- in 1555 an 'inner council' was established
- Philip's departure in 1555 and the death of Gardiner in November 1555 allowed Paget to dominate and establish a conciliar form of government.

Clashes between Gardiner and Paget

There were clashes between Gardiner and Paget, initially over Mary's marriage, but also over the revival of the heresy laws. In April 1554 parliament rejected their reintroduction and did not agree to them until they had guarantees that monastic lands would not be restored to the Church. Many have argued that this provides clear evidence of the unpopularity of Mary's religious policies. However, the struggle to reintroduce them was part of the factional struggle between Paget and Gardiner, because the same legislation that had initially been rejected was passed once Paget and his supporters backed it.

However, despite the delay in introducing the legislation and the desire of Gardiner and Paget to persuade the Queen to support their policies, they were able to put aside their differences for much of the reign.

The impact of Pole

It could be argued that the arrival of **Cardinal Pole** as **papal legate** changed the nature of court politics. It has been argued that Mary was aware of the divisions among her councillors and therefore she had everything referred to him, or to the Spanish ambassador, Simon Renard, as she did not trust her councillors' advice.

However, debates over policy in the Privy Council were usually constructive and faction should not be viewed as a bad thing; after all her half-sister, Elizabeth, was able to use it to great effect to control government by playing one group off against the other. As with Edward's reign there is no evidence to suggest that the struggles created inefficiency or prevented the government and administration from working.

Support or challenge? **a**

Below is an exam question which asks you a specific statement. Look at Sources A–D and decide whether the sources support or challenge the view. Fill in the boxes in the table below showing which statements in the source support or challenge the view. This is the first stage in answering the question and will not by itself gain high marks.

> Using these four sources in their historical context, assess how far they support the view that Mary's government was weak and divided.

Source	Support	Challenge
A		
B		
C		
D		

SOURCE A

Mary rallies support against Wyatt in a speech, 1 February 1554.

At my coronation, when I was wedded to the realm, you promised to obey me. If a Prince may as earnestly love her subjects as a mother loves her child, then be sure that I, your lady and mistress, love and favour you as tenderly. Thus loving you, I must think that you love me as faithfully; so I am sure we shall speedily overthrow these rebels.

SOURCE B

The imperial ambassador writes to the Emperor Charles about English politics in 1554.

No attention is paid to the law; the Queen and her Council are neither respected nor obeyed nor feared. The people say King Philip is not going to employ Englishmen, though he agreed to do so in the marriage treaty. They proclaim that they are to be enslaved, for the Queen is a Spanish woman at heart.

SOURCE C

The Venetian ambassador gives an assessment of developments in England during Mary's reign, May 1557.

Knowing of the divisions among her councillors, the Queen, in order not to be deceived, ordered that Cardinal Pole should have everything referred to him, since she trusts him and distrusts almost all others. The Queen is greatly grieved by the conspiracies and plots formed against her daily. When she punishes the ringleaders, she provokes hatred since the offenders are excused by almost everyone.

SOURCE D

A modern historian assesses Mary's rule. From Glyn Redworth, Female Monarchy under Philip and Mary *(1997).*

At the beginning of her reign, Mary was a strong and decisive monarch. As her reign progressed, however, Mary's weakness became more apparent. Hit by illness and phantom pregnancies, the Queen was seen as less able of imposing her will. The rivalry among her councillors is justifiably legendary. Meanwhile, Philip exercised effective control over his wife's choice of councillors.

Add your own knowledge

Annotate Sources A–D with your own knowledge to add evidence that either supports or challenges the views presented in each source about whether Mary's government was weak and divided.

Exam focus (A-level)

Below are an exam-style A-level question and model answer. Read them and the comments around the answer.

Using these four sources in their historical context, assess how far they support the view that female rule was a serious problem in the 1550s.

SOURCE A

Edward VI issues his 'Devise for the Succession' (1553) setting out who shall succeed to the crown in the event of his death.

As Lady Mary and Lady Elizabeth are both illegitimate they have no claim to the crown. As half blood to us, they would be barred by ancient law and custom of this realm and could not succeed us even if legitimate. Were the said Mary or Elizabeth to have the crown of England and marry a foreigner, he would practise his own country's laws and customs within this realm. This would utterly subvert the commonwealth of this our realm. We therefore declare that the crown shall, for lack of issue of our body, come firstly to the eldest son of Lady Frances Grey or, secondly, to the Lady Jane Grey and her male heirs.

SOURCE B

Having disregarded her Council's advice to leave the capital for her own protection, Queen Mary addresses the citizens of London on 1 February 1554 to rally their support against Wyatt's approaching rebels.

At my coronation, when I was wedded to this realm, you promised to obey me. If a Prince may earnestly love her subjects as a mother loves her child, then be sure that I, your lady mistress, love and favour you as tenderly. Thus loving you, I must think that you love me as faithfully; so I am sure we shall speedily overthrow these rebels.

SOURCE C

The Act of Parliament for a marriage treaty between Mary I and Prince Philip of Spain sets out the terms to protect English interests, 1554.

This treaty greatly honours and benefits England. The prince shall enjoy, jointly, the style and honour of king. He shall happily help administer England, preserving its rights, laws, privileges and customs. The Queen shall have total control of all offices, lands and revenues, and grant them to natural born Englishmen. Sincere friendship with Spain will be happily established forever, God willing, to benefit their successors. Should no children be born and the Queen die before him, he shall accept the lawful heir. The prince shall take no jewels abroad, nor ships, guns or supplies. He shall renew defences of the realm. By this marriage, England shall not be entangled in war, and the prince shall observe England's peace with France.

SOURCE D

A Scottish Calvinist preacher, John Knox, expresses his opinion on female rule (from The First Blast and Trumpet Against the Monstrous Regiment of Women, 1558).

To promote a woman to rule a nation is unnatural and insulting to God as contrary to his revealed will and law. It is the subversion of good order and justice. No-one can deny that it is repugnant to nature that the blind shall lead those who can see, the weak protect the strong, or the foolish and mad govern the discreet and give counsel to those of sober mind. Such are all women compared to man in bearing authority. For as rulers, their sight is blindness; their strength, weakness; their advice, foolishness; and their judgement, frenzy.

Sources D and C suggest that female rule could be a serious problem, whereas Sources A and B do not consider it a serious problem, with Source A more concerned about the question of legitimacy, while Source B does not see female rule as problem because, according to Mary Tudor, her subjects promised to obey her at her coronation.

The sources are grouped according to their view about the issue in the question.

Source D appears to offer the strongest argument that female rule was a serious problem. Knox argues that female rule was 'unnatural and insulting to God' and subverts 'good order and justice'. Written in 1558, it could be argued that there was some validity to Knox's view as he had experience of the reigns of both Mary Tudor in England and Mary Queen of Scots and neither appeared to have brought stability to their countries. England had witnessed unrest in 1554 with Wyatt's rebellion and Mary Queen of Scots was driven out of Scotland. However, it is unlikely that Knox's view was typical of views in England as many, particularly those of a Protestant or reformist outlook, supported Elizabeth. Moreover, most expected Elizabeth to marry and therefore Knox's concerns in his last sentence that as a ruler her 'sight is blindness', 'strength, weakness', 'advice, foolishness' and 'judgement, frenzy' would not have applied as she would be guided by her husband.

The source is evaluated using own knowledge which is accurate and relevant, but not developed excessively.

This view is further developed and linked to events in 1558.

Although Source C appears to suggest that female rule could be a serious problem given the for parliament to pass an Act of Parliament for a marriage treaty between Mary and Philip, it could also be argued that as parliament was able to limit Philip's power in England it was less of an issue. There were obviously concerns about a female ruler being dominated by their husband, particularly a foreigner and one as powerful as Philip, hence the restrictions placed on his power, with the Queen having 'total control of all offices, lands and revenues, and grant them to natural born Englishmen'. The source also makes it clear that parliament was concerned about being dragged into wars because of the marriage and again took measure to ensure this would not happen. However, despite the treaty England was drawn into war against France and Spanish influence did become a problem, suggesting that even with the Act female rule was a problem. Parliament might impose detailed restrictions, as Source C shows, but the problem was enforcing them. Therefore, although parliament might attempt to impose restrictions, in practice they did not work, suggesting it was a serious problem.

There is a balanced discussion about the view of the source in relation to the question.

Precise evidence of England being drawn into the Franco-Habsburg wars is used.

However, Sources A and B are less concerned about the problem of a female ruler. Source A's focus is on the problem of the legitimacy of the ruler. The Devise is more concerned about the legitimacy of Mary and Elizabeth, although it also acknowledges the problems there would be if either came to the throne and married a foreigner as he would 'practise his own country's laws' and 'subvert the commonwealth of this our realm'. However, the source has greater concerns than a female ruler as Lady Jane Grey is put forward as a possible heir, and when the Devise was later altered she was actually named as heir. However, the source was written either by Northumberland, who had personal reasons to exclude Mary and Elizabeth so as to maintain his influence, or was written by Edward who, for religious reasons, wanted to exclude Mary so that Protestantism would continue. This therefore raises questions about its reliability as its purpose was to justify excluding Mary and Elizabeth. Similarly, Source B does not see female rule as a problem, but the source was written by Mary herself and was designed to rally support for her when she was under threat from Wyatt's rebellion. According to the source female rule was not a problem as not only had the people sworn at her coronation to 'obey me', but she also argues that 'we shall speedily overthrow these rebels', suggesting that even with a female ruler a rebellion could easily be put down.

The concern of the source is explained in relation to the question and own knowledge is again applied.

The provenance of the source is used to challenge the view from earlier in the paragraph.

The source also challenges the view in Source D that a woman ruler was the equivalent of the weak leading the strong as in this instance it is Mary who is being strong and disregarding the Council's advice to leave London. There is also some justification in Mary's words as her speech did much to rally support and Wyatt was stopped soon after this speech at the gates of the city, suggesting that one of the concerns about female rulers – namely the problem of dealing with unrest – was unjustified. However, one of the causes of the rebellion was Mary's decision to marry and, as Source C shows, there were problems in having a female ruler as she was expected to marry but there was the problem of who she should marry and limiting their power.

The sources suggest that there were potential problems of having a female ruler, not simply as Source D argues because it was unnatural but because of who they should marry and the powers that the husband would have. However, as Source A suggests, there were other problems, such as legitimacy, which were also a concern and probably more so as it allowed Lady Jane to be named as a possible heir. The support there was from many for Elizabeth also suggests that Source D exaggerates the concerns about female rulers.

> The source is cross-referenced with Source D, but own knowledge is also used to evaluate it.

> A judgement is reached based on the sources, not own knowledge and it is briefly supported.

The response is focused on the question of a 'serious problem' and reaches an overall judgement as to whether the sources support the view. The sources are evaluated and own knowledge is used to place them in context and evaluate the views they offer. The response is driven by the sources and their provenance is fully considered in reaching a judgement about their reliability. The response would reach the higher levels.

What makes a good answer?

Make a list of the characteristics that make a good answer. Use the example and comments above to help you.

Below are an exam-style AS question and model answer. Read them and the comments around the answer.

Use your knowledge of Mary's reign, 1553–58, to assess how useful Source C (page 66) is as evidence for the views on a foreign marriage to a female ruler.

The source suggests that rather than there being problems with the marriage of a female ruler, in this case Mary Tudor, to a foreigner, there are many benefits. The source attempts to address the concerns that because of the sixteenth-century attitude that a wife, even a Queen, was subservient to her husband, marriage to a foreigner would lead to them dominating the country. Although the foreign prince will have the 'style and honour of king' and will help administer England, the Queen will have total control of offices, lands and revenues. The treaty attempted to address the concerns in England, shown with both the plotting of Wyatt and other rebels once the possibility of marriage became known, and the concerns and struggles in Mary's Council between Paget and Gardiner, that a foreign marriage would lead to England being dominated by foreigners and that England would become a pawn for the Habsburgs. The source acknowledges some of these concerns as it stresses that England will not become 'entangled in war', although later events that led to the loss of Calais show that this claim was incorrect. There were also concerns about the succession and that Philip might try to take the throne if no heirs resulted from the marriage, but in this instance the treaty was observed and Elizabeth succeeded without difficulties. The source does suggest that England will benefit from the friendship with Spain and, although this was the intention, the death of Mary in 1558 brought the close relationship to an end. The source also attempts to overcome the fears that were present in England that a foreign marriage would lead to patronage being in the hands of foreigners and this was certainly a concern of Wyatt, who had loyally served previous monarchs. There were also rumours circulating in England about the arrival of Spanish troops and the source may be an attempt to address the concerns about the behaviour of the troops and the reduction of England to Spanish servitude.

However, although the source attempts to address the concerns there were in England about the marriage of a female to a foreign ruler, the nature of the source, being an Act of Parliament, means that it will attempt to justify the marriage. The source's purpose was to try and allay the fears there were in England and therefore it will claim that the problems of a foreign marriage, particularly as Mary was determined to marry Philip, were exaggerated and instead would bring the Queen support and security, and it will therefore stress the benefits. It will therefore look at only the gains that England, at least in theory, would get from the marriage. Although it addresses some of the concerns, its purpose of reassuring people limits its usefulness as evidence for what would happen in practice. However, it does show how Mary attempted to justify the marriage to her subjects and reassure them.

The source is placed in the context of sixteenth-century attitudes and the concerns that would naturally arise.

Own knowledge is applied directly to the source to explain the concerns and opposition to the marriage that the treaty was designed to overcome.

Some concerns are developed and knowledge is applied to show that they were justified.

Further concerns that are tackled in the source are explained and knowledge used to explain why these issues needed addressing.

The response deals with the issue of provenance, which it is argued limits its utility.

A judgement as to its utility is developed based on the provenance of the source.

The response addresses the question and considers both the provenance of the source and uses own knowledge to test its utility. Although both elements are discussed and a judgement reached, the provenance could have been further developed in order to explain the limits to the utility of the source and this would also allow the judgement to be further developed. However, all the requirements of the mark scheme have been addressed, at least in part, and therefore the answer would reach a high level.

Exam question activity

Rewrite the last paragraph to develop the provenance and judgement in order that the answer would be awarded full marks. Use the mark scheme on page 7 to help you.

6 Religious changes

Religious policies under Edward
REVISED

Although Edward VI was a minor when he came to the throne, it was soon obvious that he had strong Protestant tendencies. Moves towards Protestantism were made easier by the nature and composition of the Regency Council that ran the country. However, support for Protestantism was not particularly strong within the country and there was still a great deal of support for traditional Catholic practices. As a result, moves towards a more reformed religion were quite slow.

Religious change could be split into the following phases during Edward's reign:
- 1547: attack on Catholicism.
- 1548: the lack of an official doctrine, but a period of uncontrolled radical Protestant activity.
- 1549–52: the establishment of Protestant worship.
- 1553: the establishment of a fully reformed Church.

The attack on Catholicism, 1547

Somerset's policy was slow and cautious – not only was the country still Catholic, but he was only a moderate Protestant. The bishops were divided and most parish clergy and the population were opposed to change. The government began by examining the condition of the Church through a royal visitation. In July 1547 the Book of Homilies, giving model sermons, and Erasmus' Paraphrases were introduced into all churches. Clergy were ordered to conduct services in English and ensure there was an English Bible present and remove superstitious images. Chantries were dissolved when parliament met, a further attack on superstition as they were places where masses for the souls of the dead were said. Parliament also repealed the Treason Act, thus lifting restrictions on what could be said, which meant radicals were free to discuss more radical reforms.

Radical activity, 1548

The abolition of the Treason Act unleashed more radical views and unrest, followed by iconoclastic attacks on altars and images. Pamphlets attacking the mass were published. As a result of these developments the government had to issue a series of proclamations between January and April 1548 to restore order and limit those who could preach. The impact of these bans was limited as in September 1548 the Council had to ban all public preaching. However, the success of the campaign against the Scots meant that the position of the government was strengthened and therefore more Protestant measures could be brought in during the autumn of 1548.

The establishment of Protestant worship, 1549–52

The Act of Uniformity was passed in January 1549 and this ordered the use of a number of Protestant practices:
- Sacraments were just communion, baptism, confirmation, marriage and burial.
- Clergy could marry.
- Singing for the souls of the dead was ended.
- Holy communion, matins and evensong were in English.
- Laity could take communion in both kinds.

However, some Catholic practices still remained. A new Prayer Book was also brought in and, despite its moderate nature, it created unrest (see pages 88), but with the fall of Somerset religious change increased in pace; attacks on images were increased, a new Ordinal was brought in in January 1550, conservative bishops were removed, a new Treason Act was brought in, stone altars were replaced by wooden tables and this was followed by a Second Act of Uniformity.

The establishment of a fully reformed Church, 1553

The Second Prayer Book and Act of Uniformity were introduced. The latter was more Protestant than the first, removing all traces of Catholicism, establishing Calvin's concept of a spiritual presence and becoming the basis for all services, but although it was used it did not mean everyone accepted the views. The Forty-Two Articles, outlining doctrine and belief, were drawn up, but never became law because of Edward's death. Therefore, upon Edward's death in 1553, England was legally Protestant.

Add your own knowledge

Below are an exam-style question and Sources A–D:
- In one colour, draw links between the sources to show ways in which they agree that the Edwardian reformation was slow and incomplete.
- In another colour, draw links where they disagree.
- Around the edge of the sources, add your own relevant knowledge. Again, draw links to show the ways in which this knowledge agrees or disagrees with the sources.

Using these four sources in their historical context, assess how far they support the view that the Edwardian reformation was slow and incomplete.

SOURCE A

Cranmer offers a fairly traditional version of communion in the Book of Common Prayer, 1549.

Grant us therefore gracious Lord so to eat the flesh of your dear son Jesus Christ, and to drink his blood, that we may continually dwell in him, and he in us. Amen.

And the minister, delivering the Sacrament of the body of Christ shall say:

The body of our Lord Jesus Christ which is given for you, preserve your body and soul unto everlasting life.

And the minister, delivering the Sacrament of the blood and giving it to everyone to drink, shall say:

The blood of our Lord Jesus Christ which was shed for you, preserve your body and soul unto everlasting life.

SOURCE B

Parliament condemns Catholic service books and images, 1550.

The King has issued through parliament a uniform, quietly and goodly order of service called the Book of Common Prayer, which contains nothing but the very pure word of God. However, alongside it are still practised corrupt, untrue and superstitious ceremonies, which allow some to attack the order and meaning of the Prayer Book and encouraged great diversity of opinion. Therefore it is ordered that all books used for the old mass be abolished, and any images of stone, timber or marble be defaced and destroyed.

SOURCE C

A bishop outlines some measures he wants priests in his diocese to follow, 1552.

You must teach that the salvation of people results from faith in Jesus Christ, not by the merit of good works.

You must condemn the idea of prayers for the dead and worshipping of saints and images.

You must teach that at communion there is no changing of the bread and wine into the body and blood of Jesus Christ.

SOURCE D

Cranmer rewrites the communion service in the Book of Common Prayer, 1552.

Hear us O merciful Father we beg you; and grant that we, receiving these your gifts of bread and wine, according to Christ's example, in remembrance of his death, may share in his most blessed body and blood.

And when the minister delivers the bread, he shall say:

Take and eat this, in remembrance that Christ died for you, and feed on him in your heart by faith, with thanksgiving.

And when the minister delivers the cup, he shall say:

Drink this in remembrance that Christ's blood was shed for you, and be thankful.

Support and opposition for the policies under Edward

Although England was officially Protestant when Edward died in 1553, it did not mean that people actively supported the religious changes of Somerset and Northumberland. Moreover, England was still Catholic when Henry died in 1547 and it is unlikely that the religious beliefs of the English people would have been changed by 1553. Even legislation, such as the Second Act of Uniformity and the Second Prayer Book, that made England a fully Protestant country was brought in only during the last year of Edward's reign so had little time to have an impact, while the Forty-Two Articles never became law.

Despite these problems, many churchwarden accounts suggest that the reforms had been carried out, altars had been replaced and the new service books were being used. However, imposing the changes was not easy and this is shown by the legislation to remove images:

- July 1547: royal injunctions ordered the removal of superstitious images.
- February 1548: all images were to be removed.
- December 1548: a proclamation ordered all remaining images to be destroyed.

The amount of legislation needed suggests that even this task was not straightforward.

Religious unrest

It is difficult to argue against the view that the Western rebellion of 1549 in Devon and Cornwall was religiously motivated. Most of the demands were religious and the rising had begun in Devon at Sampford Courtenay in June 1549, when the parishioners had demanded that the priest use the old Prayer Book, not the new version, to say mass. The rebels demanded:

- the restoration of the Six Articles
- mass in Latin
- holy bread and water, palms and ashes all to be restored
- images to be restored
- prayers for the souls of the dead.

The demands were dominated by the insistence that traditional practices were restored, although there was no demand for the restoration of papal authority.

However, it was not just in the West Country that there was religious unrest. The rising in Yorkshire at Seamer was largely triggered by religious grievances, as was unrest in Oxfordshire and Hampshire. However, Kett's rebellion in East Anglia (see page 88) wanted the religious changes to go at a faster pace.

The evidence of wills

Although evidence from wills is difficult to interpret, it appears that they show little support for the changes except in London, the south-east and East Anglia. Yet even in Kent preambles to wills show that only 8 per cent were Protestant in 1549; it was slightly better in Suffolk, with 27 per cent for the whole of Edward's reign. But this can be contrasted with York and the south-west. In York there were just two Protestant wills before 1550 and one in the south-west, suggesting that traditional religion still had much appeal, which would also make Mary Tudor's task that much easier.

Local reactions

Although the evidence of wills suggests little support for the reformed faith, there were some parishes where changes were welcomed, and it is unlikely that the new Prayer Book had no impact. However, the amount of change had probably left many confused or indifferent, with many simply conforming because they were told they had to. This also appears to be the case with many clergy, who served Henry, Edward and Mary.

Spot the inference
a

High-level answers avoid just summarising or paraphrasing the sources, and instead make inferences from the sources. Below are a source and a series of statements. Read the source and decide which of the statements:

- make an inference from the source (I)
- paraphrase the source (P)
- summarise the source (S)
- cannot be justified from the source (X).

How useful is Source A as evidence of the difficulties of introducing religious reform?

Statement	I	P	S	X
The main reasons why the introduction of Protestantism was slow were the lack of qualified clergy and legislation				
It would be difficult to make England a Protestant nation within a short period and everything possible needs to be done to encourage the government				
There were moves towards Protestantism, encouraged by the government, who considered religious change a priority				
Bucer is concerned that not only can't the bishops agree on doctrine, but there is a lack of qualified clergy, who do little to help by reading services quickly				
The bishops state that they need parliamentary support to act but parliament has many other issues that need its attention				

SOURCE A

Martin Bucer, a German Protestant who arrived in England in 1548 and taught theology at Cambridge University, sends news of religious events in England to a leading European Protestant, John Calvin, June 1550.

The Bishops have not yet agreed on Christian doctrine, let alone rules of the Church, and very few parishes have qualified clergymen. Sometimes the clergy read the services rapidly, so that ordinary people have no more understanding of it than if it were still in Latin rather than English. When these problems are presented to the bishops, they say they cannot correct them without an Act of Parliament. Though parliament meets every year, the number of secular matters stops Church affairs being discussed. When you next write to the Duke of Somerset, you must urge him to reform the Church.

Using provenance and own knowledge

Read Source A above and consider the following question:

How useful is Source A as evidence for the difficulties of introducing religious reform?

- In using provenance to evaluate the source, who is it being written to, why would it be written, how might that affect its utility?
- In using own knowledge to evaluate the source, what was important about the circumstances in which the letter was written?

Recommended reading

Below is a list of suggested further reading on this topic:
- *England 1485–1603*, pages 123–30, Mary Dicken and Nick Fellows (2015).
- *English Reformations*, pages 168–203, Christopher Haigh (1993).
- *The Early Tudors*, pages 209–25, David Rogerson, Samantha Ellsmore and David Hudson (1993).
- *Henry VII to Mary I, 1485–1558*, pages 146–53, Roger Turvey (2015).

Religious policies under Mary

At the start of her reign Mary issued a proclamation stating that she intended to proceed cautiously in religious matters, but few had doubts that her aims were to:

- undo the religious changes made since 1529
- restore papal authority
- restore traditional Catholic practices
- re-establish monasteries
- end clerical marriage
- persecute those who did not agree with her views
- secure a long-term future for Catholicism by marrying and having an heir.

She was welcomed with enthusiasm: bells were rung and parliament opened with a mass even though it was illegal. Despite this apparent support, there were a number of difficulties, with Gardiner uncertain about restoring papal authority, Renard unsure about restoring monasteries and the Pope concerned that she would move too quickly.

Restoration of papal authority

Parliament met in October 1553, but refused to repeal the Act of Supremacy. However, it did pass an Act of Repeal which undid the changes made under Edward and restored the situation to that of 1547 under the Act of Six Articles. Mary used the royal prerogative to suspend the Second Act of Uniformity and restored mass, which did not provoke serious opposition. However, there was some disquiet, as seen with Wyatt's rebellion (see page 92), which happened before any significant religious changes had occurred.

Restoration of Catholic practices

In the spring of 1554 royal injunctions restored some traditional Catholic practices, such as holy days, processions and ceremonies. A large number of married clergy were also deprived and Protestant bishops were removed.

The heresy laws and the Second Act of Repeal

Initial attempts to restore the heresy laws in April 1554 were rejected by parliament. They would not agree to this until guarantees were given that former monastic lands would not be restored. However, opposition was probably due more to factional conflict (see page 64) than opposition to Mary's religious policies as they were passed a few months later.

The Second Act of Repeal, which repealed all religious legislation passed since 1529, was passed in November 1554, but Mary was forced into a compromise with landowners, guaranteeing the rights of those who had bought Church land since 1536.

The heresy laws were reintroduced in 1554 and burnings started in February 1555 (see page 78).

Catholic reform

The return of Cardinal Pole to England was followed by the introduction of a number of positive measures to increase the appeal of Catholicism:

- Bishops were ordered to make regular visitations and check clerical behaviour.
- The London Synod, which stressed the importance of priests being resident and the ending of pluralism, was established.
- Pole ordered new publications, including a Catholic New Testament and Book of Homilies.
- Pole wanted **seminaries** in every diocese.

There were also attempts to control Protestant literature and increase the availability of Catholic works, with the sponsoring of sermons at St Paul's Cross and the publication of writings by writers such as Matthew Hogarde.

Doing reliability well

Below are an exam-style question, Sources A–D and a set of definitions listing common reasons why sources can be unreliable. For each source write a critical account of whether it is a reliable or unreliable piece of evidence, justifying your answer by referring to the definitions below.

> Using these four sources in their historical context, assess how far they support the view that the religious policies of Mary's reign were based mainly on reconciliation.

- **Vested interest**: the source is written so that the writer can protect his or her own power or interests.
- **Second-hand report**: the writer is not in a position to know and is relying on someone else's information.
- **Expertise**: the source is written on a subject that the author is an expert in.
- **Political bias**: the source is written by a politician and it reflects his or her political views.
- **Reputation**: the source is written to protect the writer's reputation.

Source A is reliable/unreliable as evidence for Mary's religious aims because:

_____

Source B is reliable/unreliable as evidence for Mary's religious aims because:

_____

Source C is reliable/unreliable as evidence for Mary's religious aims because:

_____

Source D is reliable/unreliable as evidence for Mary's religious aims because:

_____

SOURCE A

Mary reassures her subjects about her religious aims.

The Queen, being by the goodness of God settled in her just possession of the crown of this realm, cannot hide that religion which God and the world know she has always professed. The Queen desires the same religion to be quietly and charitably embraced by all her subjects. And yet she intends not to compel any of her subjects to attend Catholic services until such time as further decision, by common consent, may be taken. She therefore wills and commands all her good loving subjects to live together in Christian charity.

SOURCE B

The Spanish ambassador comments on laypeople owning former Church lands.

The present possessors must be reassured that they will not have to hand back these lands. Otherwise we shall never achieve the desired result. Unless Cardinal Pole takes this advice he will run great risks himself and make the whole religious question much more difficult.

SOURCE C

The imperial ambassador comments on events after Pole's arrival.

Last Sunday the Dean of St Paul's Cathedral preached a sermon about the return of lands to the Church. It was disliked since he argued that the lay owners of former Church lands should now return them, even though they had obtained permission to own them. There was a general opinion that Cardinal Pole had put the Dean up to this, but as the Dean had been sent for and reprimanded by the Council, it seems he must have acted without the knowledge of the Council or the Cardinal. The Cardinal has behaved well so far and followed your Majesty's advice.

SOURCE D

A Protestant clergyman writing in Elizabeth I's reign describes the execution of the vicar of Hadleigh, in Suffolk. From John Foxe, Acts and Monuments, published 1563.

The streets of Hadleigh were crowded on both sides. Dr Taylor's hair had been clipped, on the orders of Bishop Bonner. Holmes, yeoman of the guard, gave Dr Taylor a heavy blow on the head. Then the doctor knelt down and prayed and when he had prayed he went to the stake and kissed it. Then they bound him with chains. At last they kindled the fires. So he stood still until the man Soyce, with a weapon, struck him on the head and the corpse fell into the fire.

Attitudes to Marian policies and Catholic restoration

The reaction to the crowning of Lady Jane Grey and Mary's overthrow of her, as well as the lack of evidence for popular support for many of the Edwardian reforms, suggests that traditional religious practices were still popular. However, as the 1549 Western rebellion had shown, that does not mean there was unconditional support for the restoration of papal authority. Moreover, at least some of the support for Mary was not because of her religion, but because she was seen as the rightful ruler.

Evidence for popular support for Mary's religious policies

Mary's return to London was greeted with joy on the streets, in churches and in parliament. In Oxford chalices reappeared, and an altar and cross were set up on 23 August at St Nicholas Cole Abbey in London, where mass was said – a practice that was copied the next day in other churches in the capital. Large numbers also turned out for Mary's coronation, in stark contrast to Lady Jane Grey's. However, this reaction may have convinced Mary that the restoration of Catholicism would be easy.

Opposition in parliament

Although there was opposition in parliament to some religious changes (see page 64), this was usually not the result of religious concerns, as was the case with the heresy laws, the Aliens Act or the Second Act of Repeal, but due to factional, economic and land concerns, particularly the possibility of the loss of monastic lands which many gentry and nobility had purchased since 1536. Once they had guarantees about their security the legislation was passed.

Wyatt's rebellion

Wyatt's rebellion is sometimes seen as evidence of the unpopularity of Mary's religious policies, but it began before any serious changes had been implemented and, although the leaders had Protestant sympathies, was probably due more to Mary's proposed marriage to Philip of Spain (see page 92) than religious reasons, although the two were closely linked in the popular mind. The marriage could also strengthen Mary's position, make it easier for her to impose religious legislation, and even secure a Catholic succession, although given that Mary was already 37 that was perhaps less likely.

The Marian exiles

As the nature of the religious changes became apparent in the early months of 1554, some Protestants began to leave England. In total some 800 committed Protestants, mostly gentry, clergy and the more wealthy, left England and went into exile on the continent for the rest of Mary's reign. However, this was not really an option for the less well off. Moreover, at the start of Mary's reign, many were willing to wait and see what developments took place, with a number, correctly as it turned out, not expecting Mary's reign to be long given her age, which also raised doubts about her ability to produce an heir.

Popular support

This is seen in parishes, such as Morebath in Devon, where parishioners raised considerable sums of money to purchase vestments and other equipment needed to carry out Catholic services. Evidence would suggest that Catholic worship returned speedily to most parishes. However, some churches had been badly neglected during Edward's reign and it would take time to restore all the equipment. Yet it was not this that was the greatest obstacle to a Catholic restoration, but Mary's failure to produce an heir. The problems that Elizabeth would have in establishing a Protestant church are clear evidence of how popular most of Mary's policies actually were.

Explain the differences by using provenance

The following sources give different views about support for Mary's religious policies. Identify what the views are and explain the differences by using the provenance of the sources. Think about the circumstances, the nature of the evidence and the context.

What does Source A show about Parkyn's view of Mary's religious policies?

Why was the book written?

What was happening when the book was written?

What does Source B show about Hickman's view of Mary's religious policies?

Why was it written?

What was happening when she was writing?

How useful is Source A as evidence for Parkyn's view about the popularity of the changes?

6 Religious changes

SOURCE A

A Yorkshire priest records reactions of the clergy to the restoration of Roman Catholic services at the start of Mary's reign. From Robert Parkyn, Narrative of the Reformation, 1553.

In August, Queen Mary issued a proclamation licensing priests to say mass in Latin after the ancient custom used in her father's day. Then the holy church began to rejoice, singing praise to god with heart and tongue. But many heretics did not rejoice at all. It was a joy to hear and see those sinful priests who had lived their lives immorally with their whores look so dismayed. They were commanded to forsake their mistresses and do open penance according to the canon law, which then took effect.

SOURCE B

A committed Protestant and wife of a wealthy merchant recalls her experiences early in Mary's reign, writing in old age under Elizabeth. From Ross Hickman, Memoir of Protestant Life under Mary I, 1610.

When Queen Mary came to the crown, the idolatrous mass was established and cruel persecution began of good Christians who refused to accept popery. We sheltered many in our house in London. My husband smuggled some of these good Christians overseas, helping them with money. When it was proclaimed that everyone should receive the popish sacrament, I went to the bishops who were imprisoned in Oxford and later martyred, to ask whether my child should be baptised by the popish ritual. They said that he could, but advised me rather to go overseas. Afterwards I left for Antwerp.

 Using your own knowledge

In order to find evidence for a possible source-based question on the popularity of Mary's religious policies, write two extended paragraphs using your own knowledge and material from this chapter.
- Paragraph one should show the popularity of Mary's religious policies and include four examples of popularity.
- Paragraph two should show the unpopularity of Mary's religious policies and include four examples of the lack of popularity.

Catholic persecution

It is the reintroduction of the heresy laws that is the most remembered policy of Mary, reflected in her nickname of 'Bloody Mary'. During the period following the first burning, that of John Rogers in February 1555, nearly 300 went to the stake, of whom 51 were women, with most of the burnings in the south-east, London, Canterbury and Colchester. According to some accounts it lost Mary support as many, such as the fisherman Rawlins White, were ordinary citizens. However, views have been coloured by the writings of the Protestant, John Foxe, written during Elizabeth's reign.

John Foxe and his impact

The burnings are largely remembered because of John Foxe's *Acts and Monuments* (1563), more commonly known as *The Book of Martyrs*. It is this that has influenced the understanding and impact of the events, suggesting that there was widespread opposition to the regime and that it was the fires of Smithfield that turned England Protestant. Some have argued that those who actually attended the burnings were so impressed by the dedication of those being burnt that they themselves converted. However, evidence to support this claim is limited and only one person appears to have been so moved as to convert.

The impact of the burnings

Historians have also challenged Foxe's view, even though the Spanish ambassador at the time expressed concern about the impact of the burnings and feared it would cause unrest.

In October 1555, Bishops Ridley and Latimer were burnt at Oxford, followed in March 1556 by the burning of Cranmer. Although for Mary the burning of the man who had ended her mother's marriage to Henry and supported Lady Jane Grey might be seen as necessary, some have argued it was her biggest error. Cranmer had committed treason in supporting Lady Jane Grey and could have been executed: his burning gave him the chance to withdraw his previous recantations once it was apparent he would not be spared and such was his courage that his burning would not have helped the Catholic cause.

The death of Gardiner in November 1555 removed a restraining influence on Mary. Initially he had supported the persecutions, but he became aware that they were not working and might be hardening opposition. His death was followed by an increase, with some 274 perishing in the last three years of her reign.

Large numbers of people attended the burnings, and they were usually seen as spectacles. Some, such as the cherry pickers from Kent, even welcomed them as it gave them an increased market to which they could sell their produce. Although London magistrates had to order the burnings to take place early in the day so that the numbers attending were reduced, this is probably because of the disruption that London apprentices caused at many events, rather than support for the victims. It should also be remembered that the prosecutions occurred only because the victims had been reported and local authorities were willing to enforce the law.

The geography of the burnings

Most took place in the south-east, because that was where most Protestants were. However, it might also be because the area was closer to London and the authorities were more concerned about the dangers and put increased pressure on local authorities to act, whereas areas further away from the capital were less susceptible to such influence. This view is supported by the number of letters sent to **Justices of the Peace** (JPs) in the south urging action. Some have argued that the need for such letters is evidence they were unwilling to support the action, but other factors may also explain the delays, such as:

- the war against France in 1557
- JPs were unwilling to enforce other legislation, such as the Vagrancy Laws
- there were regular reminders to JPs to implement laws.

It is difficult to determine the impact of the burnings. The degree of damage it did to Mary's popularity is debatable. It was not a success but probably not a disaster.

Mind map

Using the information from the opposite page and your own knowledge, create a mind map that considers the scale and reaction to the Marian persecutions. Did they achieve their aim?

Add your own knowledge

Below are a question and Sources A–D.·
- In one colour, draw links between the sources to show ways in which they agree about whether the restoration of Catholicism had made much progress by the time of Mary's death.
- In another colour, draw links to show how they disagree.
- Around the edge of the source write relevant information using the mind map from the activity above, your own knowledge and the information from the page opposite.

Using these sources in their historical context, assess how far they support the view that Mary's restoration of Catholicism had made little progress by her death in 1558.

SOURCE A

The imperial ambassador describes parliament's reaction to Cardinal Pole's speech on his arrival in England in November 1554.

Yesterday, Parliament came to the unanimous decision that all the laws and statutes contrary to the Pope's authority should be repealed, the Church's authority be once more acknowledged, and the Cardinal admitted as Legate to carry out his mission. Although about 500 persons were gathered together, there was only one opposing voice, and there was no hint of making conditions about Church property.

SOURCE B

The imperial ambassador comments on the reaction in London to the burnings.

The people of London are murmuring about the cruel enforcement of the recent Acts of Parliament against heresy which has now begun, as shown publicly when a certain Rogers was burnt yesterday. Some of the onlookers wept. Others prayed to God to give them strength, persistence, and patience to bear the pain and not to convert back to Catholicism. Others gathered up the ashes and bones and wrapped them up in paper to preserve them. Yet others threatened the bishops. The haste with which the bishops have proceeded in this matter may well cause a revolt.

SOURCE C

An Elizabethan Protestant writer describes the burning of the vicar of Hadleigh, Suffolk.

Taylor was brought to Hadleigh bridge, where a poor man with five children stood. They held up their hands and he said, 'O dear father and good shepherd, Dr Taylor, God help you, just as you have often helped me and my poor children!' The streets were full on both sides with men and women of the town and country who wanted to see and bless him. When they saw his reverend and ancient face, with a long white beard, they wept and cried out 'God save you, good Dr Taylor!'

SOURCE D

The officials of churches in the diocese of Canterbury are ordered to fit out their churches for Catholic worship.

Goodnestone Church:

To provide front cloths for the altar for holy days, a canopy and veil for Lent.

To make a new lock for the font.

Goodhurst Church:

To provide two decent banners before Rogation week. To repair the chancel ceiling, and the glass windows of the church.

Exam focus

Below are an exam-style A-level question and model answer. Read them and the comments around the answer.

Using these four sources in their historical context, assess the view that the restoration of Catholicism in 1553–58 enjoyed little popular support.

SOURCE A

A Yorkshire priest records reactions of the clergy to the restoration of Roman Catholic services at the start of Mary's reign. From Robert Parkyn, Narrative of the Reformation, *1553.*

From August 1553 in many places in Yorkshire, priests were very glad to say mass in Latin, according to the fervent zeal and love they had unto God and his laws. Holy bread and water was given, altars were rebuilt, pictures and images set up once more. The English service was voluntarily laid aside and the Latin taken up again, and all without compulsion of any act or law, but merely on the wish of Queen Mary. And all the old ceremonies were used regularly, once the Lord Cardinal Pole arrived in this realm in November 1554.

SOURCE B

The accounts kept by the churchwardens of a Berkshire parish record the impact of the Marian restoration in the south of England.

1553   Payment to the stonemason for setting up again the high altar.

1554   Payment to Henry Snodman to remove a table which served in the church for the communion in the wicked time of schism.

1555   Payment to Edward Whayne for mending the clergyman's robes.

1556   Payment to attend the church inspection of my Lord Cardinal Pole. Payment in Abingdon for buying images. Payment for writing an answer to certain questions concerning Religion circulated by my Lord Cardinal Pole to certain of the clergy and Justices of the Peace.

SOURCE C

A committed Protestant and wife of a wealthy merchant recalls her experiences early in Mary's reign, writing in old age under Elizabeth. From Ross Hickman, Memoir of Protestant Life under Mary I, *1610.*

When Queen Mary came to the crown, the idolatrous mass was established and cruel persecution began of good Christians who refused to accept popery. We sheltered many in our house in London. My husband smuggled some of these good Christians overseas, helping them with money. When it was proclaimed that everyone should receive the popish sacrament, I went to the bishops who were imprisoned in Oxford and later martyred, to ask whether my child should be baptised by the popish ritual. They said that he could, but advised me rather to go overseas. Afterwards I left for Antwerp.

SOURCE D

The imperial ambassador, Simon Renard, comments on the reaction in London to the burnings.

The people of London are murmuring about the cruel enforcement of the recent Acts of Parliament against heresy which has now begun, as shown publicly when a certain Rogers was burnt yesterday. Some of the onlookers wept. Others prayed to God to give them strength, persistence, and patience to bear the pain and not to convert back to Catholicism. Others gathered up the ashes and bones and wrapped them up in paper to preserve them. Yet others threatened the bishops. The haste with which the bishops have proceeded in this matter may well cause a revolt. If the people got the upper hand, not only would the cause of religion be again threatened, but the persons of your Majesty and the Queen might be in peril.

Sources A and B appear to challenge the view that the restoration of Catholicism enjoyed little popular support, while Sources C and D suggest that there was both opposition and the fear of unrest because of some of the policies pursued by Mary's government. However, the nature of some of the sources suggests that such a view might be simplistic and the restoration enjoyed popular support.

The sources are usefully grouped together to give a structure to the answer.

Source A argues that not only was the restoration of Catholicism quick, but it was also popular as 'the English service was voluntarily laid aside and the Latin taken up again, and all without compulsion'. Not only that but all the old ceremonies were being used by the end of 1554 – just over a year after Mary's accession. Although Parkyn's account is based on the north of England, where Catholicism had been traditionally strong, as was seen in the reaction to the closure of the smaller monasteries in 1536 and to the formula of wills under both Henry and Edward, evidence from Melton Mowbray where the bells were rung to greet Mary's accession or in parliament where a mass was said before it was law suggest that his account was not untypical, even though he was a firm supporter of Catholicism. This is further reinforced by the restoration of images and pictures, as well as altars being rebuilt, and while his account shows that this was in the north of England, evidence from Morebath in the West Country and from Source B would reinforce such a view, even if it was slower in the south. It should also be remembered that this was quite a remarkable achievement given the cost of the restoration of many of these items, although there is also evidence that some had been hidden during Edward's reign so were readily available when Mary came to the throne, further supporting the view that people welcomed her coming to the throne knowing that she would restore Catholicism.

Source A is thoroughly evaluated in relation to the question. Detailed own knowledge is directly applied to the source and the issue of provenance is also considered. The link with Source B helps to reinforce the point that it was not just in the north that restoration occurred.

Source B adds to this view and shows that the restoration of Catholic items, even in a parish in the south of England, where Protestantism might be stronger, still took place. However, the process was slower here and with Source A might suggest there was some regional variation, but again given the cost of restoring some of the items listed, such as images, progress within the first three years of Mary's reign was still encouraging. Although the source is a simple account of the money spent by the Church to restore Catholic ritual, there is the suggestion that it was also sympathetic to the restoration as it refers to the earlier period as that 'wicked time of schism', which if it is an accurate indication of the views in the south of England, suggests the restoration was popular. This is further supported by evidence from wills from the south, which show only 20 per cent of London wills at the end of Edward's reign having a Protestant direction, further supporting the argument that Catholicism was still popular.

The link between Sources B and A is further developed to reinforce the point and provide a picture across the country. However, as with Source A, Source B is considered in a balanced manner, with acknowledgement that the process was slower.

This view is, however, challenged to some extent by Sources C and D. Source C certainly suggests that there was opposition to Catholicism as people fled the country because of its restoration. While some 800 did go into exile that figure does not suggest great unpopularity, although it must be remembered that only the wealthy would be able to afford the option. Hickman does also suggest that there were some clergy who supported Protestantism, but this source was written by a devout Protestant who was not only concerned about having her child baptised by a Catholic priest, but herself went into exile, suggesting her view of events may not be representative of most. She is also looking back during Elizabeth's reign at events under Mary and may therefore view them rather differently, contrasting the triumph of the reformed religion under Elizabeth with the bad days of Mary and her 'idolatrous mass'.

However, Source D appears to reinforce the view that there was opposition and the restoration was unwelcome and according to the imperial ambassador was bringing England close to revolt. Despite Renard's view that the burnings were causing opposition, there is actually little evidence to support his claim and he may well be exaggerating the issue to try and persuade Philip to return to England, particularly as Philip had already cautioned Mary about the implementation of the heresy laws. As ambassador, Renard's knowledge of events outside the capital would also have been limited and therefore while there might be some truth that people murmured in London there is no evidence of serious unrest at the burnings. It is true that in London the burnings had to take place early in the morning because of fears of unrest from the London apprentices, but they were often causing trouble and their activities should not be seen as an indicator that there was unpopularity. It should also be remembered that, despite Renard's comments, the only reason anyone was burnt was because they had been reported and prosecuted – further evidence that there were people who were willing to inform against the religious beliefs of their neighbours, and further evidence that the informers supported the Catholic faith. Renard also suggests that there were Protestants present who encouraged those being burnt to remain strong in their faith, and while that might be true, there were also many more who attended the burnings as entertainment – certainly the Kent cherry growers made large sums of money selling their wares at the events, difficult as that might be to understand today. It should also be remembered that the heresy laws had been passed by parliament, further suggesting that Renard's view about the unpopularity of the measure is unfounded.

Although Sources C and D suggest that there was opposition, the nature of the sources raises doubts about such a claim and, although some opposed the policy, the numbers were limited. Sources A and B offer a more accurate view of the reaction to the restoration and this is further supported by the welcome given to Mary in 1553 and the problems Elizabeth I would face from 1558 onwards in implementing a Protestant settlement both within parliament and the country.

A link between the two sources is made.

Own knowledge is used to test the provenance.

There is an impressive level of own knowledge used to test the view in the source.

Sources C and D are treated together. The question of the provenance of both is considered and knowledge is also applied to explain the limitations of both sources in terms of the question.

The judgement is based on the sources and this is supported by some brief but relevant contextual own knowledge.

The response is focused on the question and although the sources are treated discretely, there is some cross-referencing which is used effectively to take the argument forward. The sources are all evaluated using both provenance and own knowledge, with some of the own knowledge being quite detailed, but it is used and linked to the actual source under discussion and not simply imparted. The judgement is based on the sources and therefore, given both provenance and own knowledge are used effectively, the response will reach the higher levels.

> **Working with the sources**
>
> In different colours, underline examples where the answer uses own knowledge, evaluates, cross-references and quotes from the sources.

AS-level question

Read Source E and answer the following question:

Use your knowledge of religious changes under Mary to assess how useful Source E is as evidence of opposition to Mary I's religious policies.

SOURCE E

A royal messenger, and cousin of a former Lord Chancellor, records an eyewitness account of an event in London, April 1554.

On Sunday a villainous event took place in Cheapside. A dead cat was hanged on the post of gallows, dressed in cloth like the vestment of a priest at mass with crosses front and back. Its head was shaved, a bottle was nearby and between its front paws was a piece of paper like a consecrated wafer. It was taken to bishop Bonner of London, who showed it to the audience attending the sermon at St Paul's Cross. The Lord Mayor offered a reward to anyone naming the culprit. Inquiries were made and several persons were imprisoned under suspicion.

7 Rebellion and unrest

Causes of the unrest, 1547–58

The period from the death of Henry VIII in 1547 to the death of Mary Tudor in 1558 witnessed a large number of rebellions, and an even greater number of local riots and smaller outbreaks of unrest. There were a number of causes of the unrest.

Social and economic problems

Social and economic issues were often an underlying cause of the unrest and included issues such as:

- population growth
- rising prices
- poor harvests
- increasing poverty
- enclosure.

However, although these problems were becoming more acute, they were seldom the trigger for unrest (see page 88). Nevertheless, some of the issues, particularly enclosure, did play a significant role in the outbreak of Kett's rebellion in 1549 and had started earlier unrest at Northaw in Hertfordshire in 1548. The issue of enclosure led to the establishment of an Enclosure Commission by Somerset and this convinced many peasants that he was sympathetic to their cause and may have encouraged the unrest in the summer of 1549 that gripped much of central and southern England.

Factional and political causes

The accession of a minor, Edward VI, increased factional conflicts within government. As Edward was only a minor this meant that the government was in the hands of a group of councillors, the Regency Council. Members of the Council looked to increase their influence and also sought to increase their personal wealth. This was seen in the struggle in 1549 and the early months of 1550 when Somerset was removed from power by a coup and Northumberland succeeded him and became Lord President of the Council. The factional struggle continued; Somerset attempted to regain his influence until he was executed in 1552.

This was not the end of the political struggles as Northumberland attempted to retain influence upon the death of Edward VI in 1553 by placing Lady Jane Grey on the throne, which brought England close to civil war (see page 90) and then after the defeat of this coup, Mary Tudor's reign also witnessed factional conflict. There were attempts by some councillors to dissuade Mary from marrying Philip of Spain as they feared losing influence to Spaniards and this encouraged Wyatt's rebellion of 1554 (see page 92). It can therefore be seen that the presence of first a minor and then a woman on the throne contributed to unrest.

Religious change

Religious uncertainty caused by the changes under Henry VIII added to the potential for instability. This was first seen in 1547 and 1548 in Cornwall when William Body attempted to supervise the destruction of images. The introduction of a new Prayer Book in 1549 led to the Western or Prayer Book rebellion in 1549 as people in the West Country complained about the abolition of traditional religious practices, and even Kett's rebels had some religious grievances. However, unlike the Western rebels, their demands were for further moves towards Protestantism, rather than its abandonment.

The potential restoration of Catholicism by Mary may have played a role in Northumberland's decision to try and put the Protestant Lady Jane Grey on the throne and similarly Wyatt may have rebelled because he did not want a Catholic regime. However, there is evidence to suggest that these rebellions were more factional and political in nature.

Spot the inference

High-level answers avoid just summarising or paraphrasing the sources, and instead make inferences from the sources. Below are a source and a series of statements. Read Source A and decide which of the statements:

- make an inference from the source (I)
- paraphrase the source (P)
- summarise the source (S)
- cannot be justified from the source (X).

How useful is Source A as evidence for the causes of unrest in England in 1549?

Statement	I	P	S	X
The risings have spread and could be a threat. The demands of the rebels are largely social and economic, with some unrealistic requests, but where handled well they can be put down quickly so are not a serious threat.				
The ambassador is saying that peasant revolts have spread to all parts of England. He says that the peasants want land to be leased to them at the same rate as it was under Henry VII. The riots in some areas ended when food was taxed at a reasonable price. He says religion is not a major cause of the unrest.				
The revolts are widespread and are caused by economic issues, such as rent and the taxes on foodstuffs, while religion is not a major cause. Some ended when the taxes on food were reduced.				
The revolts were less about social and economic issues and more about religion and political problems.				

SOURCE A

The Imperial Ambassador writes an account of the risings of 1549 to Charles V, 19 July 1549.

The revolt of the peasants has increased and spread, so that now they have risen in every part of England, asking for things just and unjust. They demand they may use the land that once used to be public property, and that land leased to them shall be considered to be of the same value now as in the time of Henry VII, who died in 1509. This last request is very difficult to meet. In Kent and Essex the risings ended when foodstuffs were taxed at a reasonable price. There is no mention of religion made among any of them, except in Cornwall and Norfolk.

Assessing reliability

How reliable is Source A as an expression of the causes of unrest in England in 1549? To help you decide, complete the table below:

When was it written?	
Why would van der Delft be eager to report the unrest in England?	
Was it a private or a public document?	
Who would read the document?	
From your own knowledge, was this typical of the explanations given for the unrest in England at this time?	

Social and economic developments

REVISED

The economic and social changes that affected England in the sixteenth century, particularly in the middle of the century, have often been seen by historians to be the underlying cause of the unrest that appeared to grip the mid Tudor period. However, many contemporaries saw the social and economic problems in more moralistic terms, often blaming landowners for being greedy.

Population rise

Contemporary writings ignored the most important underlying issue, the rise in population. For the first time since the Black Death in the fourteenth century, the population was rising. Although there are no accurate figures available, it would appear that between 1525 and 1551 it rose from 2.3 million to 3 million. This may not appear large, but it had a far-reaching impact. Agricultural productivity was unable to keep pace with the rise and therefore the price of food rose. This meant that when there were bad harvests, of which there were many in the period, it became a serious issue. Grain prices rose faster than other food prices and because it was the staple diet it had an even greater impact.

Not only did the population rise, but the structure changed. It was a young population, which meant that many were too young to work and therefore the dependency ratio increased as many were children who were consumers but not producers.

Agricultural problems and enclosure

Not only was it difficult to increase production levels of grain, as people did not have fertilisers and were not aware of crop rotation, but also many farmers were changing from arable to sheep farming as the demand for cloth grew. This created further problems because sheep farming required fewer labourers, as fewer workers were needed to look after sheep, and therefore caused unemployment.

It also encouraged another development, which was seen as an evil by many contemporary commentators: enclosure. The government of Somerset attempted to tackle the problem by establishing Enclosure Commissions in both 1548 and 1549 to look into the problem, but attempts at legislation were blocked by the gentry in parliament as they were gaining from such developments. Somerset issued proclamations to try and force landowners to reverse the development, but this lost him the support of the gentry and encouraged the lower orders to take action themselves and throw down hedges.

Price rise

Contemporaries tended to blame the rise in prices on the greed of landowners, but it was largely due to the rising population and the inability of the agricultural system to meet the growing demand for food.

Year	Price rise compared to 1508 (%)
1520	37
1530	69
1545	91
1546	148
1549	114

The situation was made worse by the debasement of the currency to finance the wars against France and Scotland in the 1540s. It meant more money was in circulation but not more food and therefore prices rose further. This was made worse by bad harvests, with six bad harvests in the period from 1547 to 1558 and those in 1548 and 1549 were little better. The poor suffered even more because the Dissolution of the Monasteries had removed the one institution that helped during difficult times.

Poverty and vagrancy

Enclosure had decreased the numbers needed in the workforce and a slump in the cloth trade only added to unemployment. The price rise also meant there was an increase in the number of poor. This worried the authorities, particularly when large numbers were concentrated together, as they lacked a force to maintain order and prevent crime. The government therefore brought in harsh measures, such as the 1547 Vagrancy Act, which condemned vagrants to slavery.

Add your own knowledge

Below are an exam-style question and Sources A–D.
- In one colour, draw links between the sources to show ways in which they agree.
- In another colour, draw links where they disagree.
- Around the edge of the sources, add your own relevant knowledge. Again, draw links to show the ways in which this knowledge agrees or disagrees with the sources.

Using these sources in their historical context, assess the view that the price rise was the main reason for the social problems in this period.

SOURCE A

A social commentator attacks the rise of oppressive landlords.

Many landlords oppress the common people. They have increased their rents, so that they charge £40 rather than £2 for a new lease, and £5 not 5 nobles (almost £2) for its annual rent, so we now pay more to them than we earn. The result is that many thousands of us who once lived honestly upon our labour must now beg, or borrow, or rob and steal, to get food for our poor wives and children. They also compel others to surrender their rights to hold leases for two or three lives and to accept instead leases for just twenty-one years.

SOURCE B

A clergyman identifies some major economic grievances.

See how rich men, especially sheep owners, oppress the King's subjects by enclosing the common pasture and filling it with their sheep. How many sheep they have! Yet when was wool so expensive, or mutton so great a price? If this goes on, the people will die of cold or starve to death. For these greedy wolves will either sell their wool and their sheep at their own high price, or else not at all. Other men buy up houses, even whole villages, and then allow them to fall into ruin and decay.

SOURCE C

An ambassador writes an account of the risings.

The revolt of the peasants has increased and spread, so that now they have risen in every part of England, asking for things just and unjust. They demand they may use the land that once used to be public property, and that land leased to them shall be considered to be of the same value now as in the time of Henry VII, who died in 1509. This last request is very difficult to meet. In Kent and Essex the risings ended when foodstuffs were taxed at a reasonable price. There is no mention of religion made among any of them, except in Cornwall and Norfolk.

SOURCE D

One of the Commonwealth writers attacks landlords for their behaviour. From Robert Crowley, The Way to Wealth, 1550.

Contrary to the law against oppression and extortion, you have enclosed from the poor their common land, levied greater entry fees payable on new leases, excluded them from their rightful use of the common land, and raised their rents. What obedience did you show when the King's proclamations were sent forth to open up your enclosures, and yet you continued to enclose? If you had loved your country, would you not have prevented the recent great destruction which followed from your incurable greed?

 Essay planning

Plan a mini-essay on this topic 'How serious were the economic problems in the period 1547–50?' Find four pieces of evidence from this book and your own reading to show that they were serious and four pieces of evidence to show they were not serious, and explain them. Write a conclusion based on these points.

The rebellions of 1549

The late spring and summer of 1549 witnessed much of central and southern England facing riot and rebellion, with at least some 25 counties affected. Most rebellions were put down by local gentry, but two – the Western and Kett's – required the use of government troops. Most of the unrest had long-term economic and social factors at the root of the problem, most notably enclosure and rising prices.

The Western rebellion

This has usually been called the Prayer Book rebellion, suggesting it was religiously motivated. Events beforehand suggest there was religious tension as William Body was murdered at Helston in 1548 when he returned to supervise the destruction of images. A large number of people gathered at Bodmin to protest about the Act of Uniformity, but the major unrest started at Sampford Courtenay on Whitsunday, where locals protested about the new Prayer Book and insisted the priest use the old one. Protest soon spread and rebels from Devon and Cornwall met at Crediton. The rebel demands were largely religious, but this was because they were probably drawn up by priests. They wanted to restore traditional doctrine and asserted a belief in transubstantiation and purgatory. However, it appears that initial complaints included an attack on the sheep and cloth tax, while the action of the rebels suggests that they disliked the local gentry:

- Gentry were attacked and robbed at St Michael's Mount.
- At Bodmin they shouted 'Kill the gentlemen'.
- They murdered William Hellyons, a member of the local gentry.
- They attacked Trematon Castle.

The rebels laid siege to Exeter, where fears that the city would be handed over to the rebels led the mayor to provide poor relief, firewood and food for the poor.

The rebels' dislike for the gentry meant that when rebellion broke out they were unable to restrain the commons and the government had to send a force under Lord John Russell. They were slow to deal with the unrest as they had to put down unrest in Oxfordshire and Buckinghamshire en route. However, when they did arrive in the West Country, a number of skirmishes occurred at Fenny Bridges, Clyst St Mary and Clyst heath, before the rebels were finally defeated at Sampford Courtenay, where some 3,000 rebels were killed and further retribution followed.

Kett's rebellion

This rebellion took place in East Anglia and took its name from its leader, Robert Kett. The unrest began as enclosure riots in the towns of Attleborough and Wymondham. The rioters were angry that a local lawyer, John Flowerdew, had bought the local abbey church and begun to enclose the land. He attempted to turn the rebels against Kett, who had also enclosed land, but he turned the rebels against Flowerdew. Kett quickly raised 16,000 men who marched to Norwich and set up a camp on Mousehold Heath. The rebels were offered a pardon, but this failed to disperse them. Instead they seized Norwich. The government sent a force under the Marquis of Northampton, but it was defeated and therefore the Duke of Northumberland was sent. His force massacred the rebels at Dussindale outside Norwich, killing some 3,000. Kett was hanged for treason but many rebels were treated leniently.

The rebel demands

These can be put under four headings:

- Agricultural demands: concern about enclosure, particularly of valuable saffron grounds, gentry abuse of the **foldcourse system** and their overstocking of common land.
- Economic concerns: rising rents.
- Social grievances: the gentry's manipulation of local government.
- Religious concerns: they wanted better preachers and further reform.

Other unrest in 1549

Evidence suggests it was caused by long-term economic changes, but also religion. There was opposition to enclosure, with rebels attacking hedges, but in Oxfordshire, Yorkshire and Hampshire it appears the religious changes were the main cause.

Doing reliability well **a**

Below are an exam-style question, Sources A–D and a set of definitions listing common reasons why sources can be unreliable. For each source write a critical account of whether it is a reliable or unreliable piece of evidence, justifying your answer by referring to the definitions below.

Using these sources in their historical context, assess the view that religion was the main cause of unrest in 1549.

- **Vested interest**: the source is written so that the writer can protect his or her own power or interests.
- **Second-hand report**: the writer is not in a position to know and is relying on someone else's information.
- **Expertise**: the source is written on a subject that the author is an expert in.
- **Political bias**: the source is written by a politician and it reflects his or her political views.
- **Reputation**: the source is written to protect the writer's reputation.

SOURCE A

On behalf of the King, the Archbishop of Canterbury replies to the demands of the Western rebels.

When I first read your request, ignorant men of Devon and Cornwall, I thought that you were deceived by some crafty papist, who devised those articles for you, to request things which you did not understand. The devisers of your articles are extreme papists, willful traitors, enemies to God, our sovereign and the whole realm. You ask for general councils and holy decrees to be restored, but these are made only for the advancement, glory and greed of the Bishop of Rome.

SOURCE B

Kett and other rebel leaders in Norfolk present their demands to the Privy Council, July 1549.

That new acts of enclosure be not hurtful to such as hath enclosed saffron grounds.

That no lord of a manor shall use the common land.

That meadow ground may be sold at such a price as it was in the first year of Henry VII's reign.

That priests should be resident in their parishes so that parishioners may be instructed in the laws of God.

SOURCE C

The Venetian ambassador in England, Matteo Dandolo, reports on the unrest and the government's response, in a letter to the Senate of Venice, 20 July 1549.

There is news of major risings against the government in England, and that the King has retreated to a strong castle outside London. The cause of this is the common land, as the great landowners occupy the pastures of the poor people. The rebels also require the return of the Mass, together with the religion as it stood on the death of Henry VIII.

SOURCE D

Protector Somerset expresses his views about the unrest to a close advisor in a letter, 24 August 1549.

Some rebels wish to pull down enclosures and parks; some want to recover their common land; others pretend religion is their motive. A number would want to rule for a time, and do as gentlemen have done, and indeed all have a great hatred of gentlemen and regard them as their enemies. The ruffians among them, and the soldiers, who are the leaders, look for loot. So the rebellions are nothing other than a plague and fury among the vilest and worst sort of men.

The Lady Jane Grey affair

The background to the plot was discussed in Chapter 5 (page 60). This section will consider whether the challenge was due to religion or politics, although contemporaries probably did not draw a distinction.

Causes of the plot

Historians have debated whether the main factor behind the plot was political or religious.

Political issues

When Northumberland's son married Lady Jane Grey in May 1553, the health of Edward was such that it was believed he would live for a long time. Northumberland therefore had little to gain politically from it. It was Edward's declining health that changed the situation. The change made to the Devise (see page 60) meant that Northumberland became the father-in-law of the prospective Queen. This suggests that Northumberland had not been plotting to further his political career.

Religious issues

Instead, religious issues should be considered. Edward was a strong Protestant and concerned about his Catholic half-sister, Mary, taking the throne.

However, once Northumberland's position changed he did attempt to secure his position, aware that his Protestant beliefs meant he was likely to be excluded by Mary. Northumberland may also have thought that he would gain support from the elite as he had restored stability after the failings of Somerset's rule and many would want that to continue. It could also be argued that those who had gained land from the Dissolution of the Monasteries might support him as they could lose those lands if there was a Catholic restoration.

The threat to Mary

Northumberland was able to have Lady Jane Grey proclaimed Queen and, if he had been able to capture Mary before she fled to East Anglia, the plot might have succeeded. Northumberland initially had the support of the Privy Council, but Mary, by raising a force, proclaiming herself Queen, issuing proclamations, letters of summons and asking Charles V for help, raised the possibility of civil war.

Northumberland lost his advantage and was forced to leave London to confront Mary, and this allowed members of the Privy Council the chance to reconsider their views. Many changed their opinion and gave their support to Mary, while Northumberland failed to gain support as he marched east, with some of his own force deserting. This forced him to abandon his march, retreat to Cambridge and proclaim Mary Queen.

Aftermath

The sudden collapse of the plot suggests that it stood no chance. This appears to be reinforced by the enthusiasm with which Mary was greeted when she entered London. Some may have feared a return to instability and therefore supported the legitimate ruler. However, it did place many who had initially supported Northumberland in a difficult position. Nevertheless, the leniency shown to many suggests that Mary considered her position weak and that she needed support:

● She soon released Gardiner and Norfolk from jail.
● She appointed Paget to the Privy Council.

However, Northumberland, Lady Jane Grey and Guildford Dudley were arrested. Northumberland was soon executed, with the others following later.

Explain the differences by using provenance

The following sources give different evidence of Mary Tudor's claim to the throne following Edward VI's death. Identify what the views are and explain the differences by using the provenance of the sources. Think about the circumstances, the nature of the evidence and the context.

What does Source A show about Mary's view of her claim?

Why and to whom was the letter sent?

Where was Mary and what position was she in when the letter was sent?

What does Source B show about Mary's claim to the throne?

Why was the letter produced and to whom was it addressed?

What was happening in London when it was written?

SOURCE A

After the announcement of Lady Jane Grey's accession, Mary writes to the Privy Council in July 1553, sending copies of the letter to many large towns.

It seems strange that you did not tell us of our brother's death on Thursday night. Yet, I rely on your loyalty, considering my status, the good of the country and all your honours. Nevertheless, we know you have assembled a force and naturally we fear some evil. But we can take these actions in gracious part, being ready to fully pardon you to avoid bloodshed and vengeance. We trust not to have to use the service of other true subjects and friends abroad whose rightful cause God shall support. We require you to proclaim our right and title to the Crown and government of this realm.

SOURCE B

The Privy Council rejects Mary's claim to the throne, 9 July 1553.

We advise you that our Sovereign Lady Queen Jane is possessed of the crown, not only by good order of old ancient records of this realm, but also by the late King Edward's letters signed with his own hand and sealed with the Great Seal of England, with nobles, councillors and judges agreeing to these letters. We must remind you that owing to the divorce between King Henry VIII and your mother, in accordance with the law of God and confirmed by Acts of Parliament [1534 and 1537] you are illegitimate and unable to inherit the crown.

Using your own knowledge

Which of these statements could be used to assess how reliable Source A is as evidence for Mary's view on her claim to the throne? Indicate by ticking the boxes in the table below.

Statement	Useful	Not useful
Edward's death was kept quiet for two days		
Prominent men in London had been forced to sign the Devise		
Mary Tudor had fled to East Anglia, where she raised forces		
The Council ordered sheriffs and justices near to London to raise forces		
Mary proclaimed herself queen the next day, issued letters of summons and asked for support from Charles V		

Wyatt's rebellion

Historians are divided over the causes of Wyatt's rebellion, with some emphasising its religious nature, while others stress that it was political and caused by Mary's decision to marry Philip of Spain.

Causes of the rebellion

The timing of the rising suggests that Mary's marriage was the main cause, as no sooner were there rumours of the match than opposition began to develop. Hatred of foreigners was easily aroused and stories soon circulated that the English court would be dominated by Spaniards. There were fears that Mary would be dominated by her husband and England would be dragged into Habsburg conflicts that did not benefit England. There were soon rumours that Mary was to be removed and replaced by her half-sister Elizabeth and by December 1553 this had turned into a plot. Wyatt's propaganda certainly stressed the issue of marriage, probably aware that it would win him greater support than religious arguments. However, his claims should be seen as propaganda as there is some evidence of religious motivation:

- The leaders of the four-pronged attack had Protestant sympathies.
- The area around Maidstone where he gained most support was Protestant.
- Wyatt received advice from the deprived Protestant Bishop of Winchester.
- No prominent member of the plot was Catholic.
- On reaching London, the rebels attacked the property of the newly restored Catholic Bishop of Winchester.

However, at the time of the plot persecution of Protestants had not started. Economic factors may have helped Wyatt win support as the Kent cloth industry was in decline.

Events

The court was aware of the plot and examined Edward Courtenay, who the plotters were going to marry to Elizabeth. He revealed most of the details and forced the rebels to act before they were fully prepared. Instead of a four-pronged attack, it was only in Kent that rebellion occurred, led by a member of the Kentish gentry, Thomas Wyatt. He had been a loyal supporter of the Tudors and supported Mary against Lady Jane Grey. He was fearful he would lose his position and influence with the arrival of large numbers of foreigners.

The appeal to xenophobia made it difficult for the regime to raise forces against Wyatt and he was able to play on the fear of what would happen when Philip arrived in England. Wyatt was able to gather a force of some 3,000 men, but instead of marching straight to London, he laid siege to Cooling Castle. This gave Mary time to rally her forces, and with a rallying speech at Guildhall she brought the rebellion to an end. However, it had been a threat to Mary:

- Troops sent to deal with Wyatt had changed sides crying 'We are all Englishmen'.
- Many waited to see what would happen and did not initially support Mary.
- The rising had been close to London.

Aftermath

The lack of punishment that followed the revolt suggests Mary feared that further punishment would provoke more unrest and may explain why both Elizabeth and Courtenay would escape with their lives. It may have been Mary's speech at Guildhall which flattered her supporters and saved her as she ignored the Council's advice to leave London, in the same way that her actions in proclaiming herself Queen in 1553 had won her the throne.

The failure of this rebellion, and others in the period, may have caused a change in outlook and made most realise that rebellion was futile, and therefore indirectly strengthened the regime.

Below are an exam-style question, Sources A–C and a set of definitions listing common reasons why sources can be unreliable. For each source write a critical account of whether it is a reliable or unreliable piece of evidence, justifying your answer by referring to the definitions below.

Using these sources in their historical context, assess the view that Wyatt's rebellion was a serious threat to Mary Tudor.

- **Vested interest**: the source is written so that the writer can protect his or her own power or interests.
- **Second-hand report**: the writer is not in a position to know and is relying on someone else's information.
- **Expertise**: the source is written on a subject that the author is an expert in.
- **Political bias**: the source is written by a politician and it reflects his or her political views.
- **Reputation**: the source is written to protect the writer's reputation.

SOURCE A

The imperial ambassador, Simon Renard, reports to the Emperor Charles V on the situation in England at the start of Wyatt's rebellion.

Wyatt's men have rebelled in Kent, proclaiming that they will not consent to a foreign marriage and that every good Englishman ought to help them fight the Spaniards. Although the rebels use the foreign marriage as an excuse, like Carew, their real causes are religion and to favour Elizabeth. It is said that the rebellion is spreading. We hear news that the French and Scots are hastily fitting out ships and raising troops to aid the rebels. We hear the King of Denmark is joining in, hoping to marry Elizabeth to his son or brother.

SOURCE B

The Queen addresses the people of London outside Guildhall as the rebels approach the city, 1 February 1554.

I come personally to tell you how traitorously and rebelliously a number of Kentish men have assembled against their sovereign and her subjects. They first pretended they opposed my marriage, but the Council have spoken to them again and it seems the marriage is merely a Spanish cloak to conceal their real purpose against our religion. My loving subjects, I am your Queen with the same royal rights as my father. You were always faithful and loving to him and therefore I do not doubt that you will be as faithful to me. I, being your lady and mistress, tenderly love and favour you in return.

SOURCE C

A well-informed contemporary outlines the major events of the rebellion. From Charles Wriothesley's Chronicle of England for 1554.

On 29 January the Duke of Norfolk tried to attack Rochester Castle, where the traitor Wyatt and his rebels lay, but he was forced to flee and the rebels captured his artillery. On 1 February Queen Mary went to the city of London, and denounced Wyatt's attempt to take her crown and sack the city. On 3 February Wyatt's army reached London Bridge. On 7 February the Earl of Pembroke gathered the royal army near at Charing Cross near the city, but Wyatt and some rebels avoided them and got close to the city, where they were captured.

Exam focus (AS-level)

Below are an exam-style AS question and model answer. Read them and the comments around the answer.

Use your knowledge of unrest in 1549 to assess how useful Source A is as evidence for the breakdown of stability.

SOURCE A

Protector Somerset expresses his views about the unrest to a close advisor in a letter, 24 August 1549.

Some rebels wish to pull down enclosures and parks; some want to recover their common land; others pretend religion is their motive. A number would want to rule for a time, and do as gentlemen have done, and indeed all have a great hatred of gentlemen and regard them as their enemies. The ruffians among them, and the soldiers, who are the leaders, look for loot. So the rebellions are nothing other than a plague and a fury among the vilest and worst sort of men.

The source provides useful evidence to suggest that stability had broken down in 1549. It explains that not only had rebels attacked enclosures, but also that the social order was under threat as there was 'a great hatred of gentlemen'. These claims are certainly supported by the actions of rebels in East Anglia, where unrest began with attacks on the enclosures of both John Flowerdew and Robert Kett, but also in other parts of the country, with fences pulled down in Surrey and contemporaries even commenting about attacks on enclosures in the West Country. The rebels in both the Western and Kett's Rebellions also showed a distinct dislike for their social superiors, which Source A suggests, as in the west they attacked gentry at St Michael's Mount and murdered William Hellyons, while in East Anglia Kett established a rebel camp at Mousehold Heath from which he organised an alternative local government. This dislike of the local gentry was further confirmed by the number of articles in their demands which complained about the role of the gentry in local government. The rebels regarded the 'gentlemen' as their enemies as none of the rebellions saw gentry or nobility on the side of the rebels, suggesting there was breakdown in stability. However, Somerset blames the breakdown purely on social issues and states that religion was not a cause, but that the rebels instead 'pretend religion is a motive', which is not correct as most of the demands of the Western rebels concerned religion and the changes he had brought in.

The source was written by Somerset and therefore as Protector, writing in a letter to a close advisor, it would be expected that not only would he know what the causes were and how serious the problems were, but that he would be able to express his views in a candid manner. However, despite this, by the end of August 1549 Somerset was fighting for his political future and therefore his explanation of the events will be to justify and attempt to improve his own position and may not reflect the actual situation. Somerset would not admit that religion was a cause because it was his religious policies that had brought about the unrest and with members of the government, gentry and nobility attacking him and his policies it is not surprising that he wanted to blame other issues and suggest that the rebellions were a 'plague and fury among the vilest and worst sort of men'.

> Precise own knowledge is directly linked to the source to support the view and suggest therefore that it is useful.

> Further detailed knowledge is applied.

> The view offered in the source is challenged and the reasons for that are developed in the next paragraph.

> There is a balanced discussion of the provenance of the source and a judgement, supported by own knowledge, is reached.

Quick quizzes at **www.hoddereducation.co.uk/myrevisionnotes**

As a result, the source is only partially useful as evidence for the breakdown in stability • ——
as it is from the leader of a government which was under severe pressure, had at one
point lost control of Norwich and been forced to send troops to put down the unrest.
However, it does show how Somerset attempted to explain the breakdown and justify
his own position.

> An overall judgement
> about the source is
> reached, which is not
> simply asserted but is
> supported.

The source is thoroughly evaluated in relation to the issue in question, using both
own knowledge and provenance, rather than just generally. A judgement about the
usefulness is reached, which is supported. The use of precise knowledge that is
directly linked to the source and consideration of the provenance would take the
response into the higher levels.

What makes a good answer?

List the characteristics of a good answer to a AS Part (a) question – see page 7.

Exam practice activity

Use your own knowledge of unrest in 1549 to assess how useful this source is
as evidence for class conflict.

SOURCE

A member of the gentry comments on the behaviour of Kett's rebels

Those gentlemen they captured they brought to the tree of Reformation where they
asked the people what they wanted to do with them: some cried hang them and some
kill them. Some, who were unable to hear, shouted like the rest and when asked why
they did that, answered they copied their fellows. They also pushed their weapons into
the gentlemen in order to kill some of those brought to them, and they did this with such
malice ... Moreover, the rest of the gentlemen they imprisoned were bound with chains
and locks and they appointed guards to prevent them from escaping.

Nicholas Sotherton, Commoyson in Norfolk, 1549.

Exam focus (A-level)

Below are four sources, an exam-style A-level question and a model answer. Read them and the comments around the answer.

Using these four sources in their historical context, assess how far they support the view that religious changes were the main cause of unrest in 1549.

SOURCE A

The King, Edward VI, in a letter written for him by Protector Somerset in July 1549, lists some of the demands of the rebels of Devon and Cornwall.

For baptism, you are fearful that your children should now only be christened on holy days. You say certain Cornishmen are offended because they do not have their service in Cornish, since they understand no English.

You object that religious changes were made without my knowledge. But I deny this and affirm that the prayer book is according to scripture and the word of God.

You require the tax granted to me by parliament on cloth and sheep be cancelled. You complain of the shortage of food and other things.

SOURCE B

From the demands of Kett's rebels in the summer of 1549.

Article 3: We pray your grace that no lord of the manor encloses the common land.

Article 5: We pray that reed ground and meadow ground are the same rent as they were in the first year of King Henry VII.

Article 8: We pray that priests or vicars that are unable to preach and set forth the word of God to their parishioners may be removed from their benefice and the parishioners chose another.

Article 10: We pray no man under the status of knight or esquire keep a dovecote, unless it has been the custom.

SOURCE C

The Venetian ambassador in England, Matteo Dandolo, reports on the unrest and the government's response, in a letter to the Senate of Venice, 20 July 1549.

There is news of major risings against the government in England, and that the King has retreated to a strong castle outside London. The cause of this is the common land, as the great landowners occupy the pastures of the poor people. The rebels also require the return of the Mass, together with religion as it stood on the death of Henry VIII. The government, wishing to apply a remedy, put upwards of 500 persons to the sword, sparing neither women nor children.

SOURCE D

Protector Somerset expresses his views about the unrest to a close advisor in a letter, 24 August 1549.

Some rebels wish to pull down enclosures and parks; some want to recover their common land; others pretend religion is their motive. A number would want to rule for a time, and do as gentlemen have done, and indeed all have a great hatred of gentlemen and regard them as their enemies. The ruffians among them, and the soldiers, who are the leaders, look for loot. So the rebellions are nothing other than a plague and a fury among the vilest and worst sort of men.

Quick quizzes at **www.hoddereducation.co.uk/myrevisionnotes**

All four sources comment on the role of religion as a cause of unrest. Source A offers the strongest argument that religion was the main cause, while Sources B and C suggest that it was a cause, along with social and economic issues, but Source D argues that religion was not a motive, but an excuse as 'others pretend religion is their motive'.

Source A has the strongest argument that religion was the main cause. Somerset, writing on behalf of the young King, acknowledges that many of the demands of the Western rebels concerned religion, noting in particular their demands on christenings and the language of the new service. This view is valid as most of the final demands drawn up the Western rebels were on religious matters, with attacks on the new Prayer Book, which they described as a 'Christmas game', and complaints about the abolition of holy water. This view is further reinforced by the timing of the rebellion, which began immediately after the moderately Protestant Prayer Book was introduced at Whitsun in 1549. However, even Somerset's response to the rebels acknowledges that religion was not the only cause as he refers to the tax on sheep and cloth as a cause. This issue was absent from the rebels' final demands and raises doubts about how far those demands reflect the actual grievances of the rebels and instead provide evidence that they only pretended that religion was their motive, as suggested in Source D, because the rising had been hijacked by the clergy. The actions of the rebels, with their attacks on the gentry, would further suggest that, despite Somerset's comments in Source A, which stress the religious nature of the rising, the initial causes also included social and economic grievances, such as enclosure and the proposed sheep tax. Somerset, as Lord Protector, would have wanted to be clear about the actual causes in addressing the rebels, and unlike Source D when his position had deteriorated because of the scale of unrest, would not have had needed to cover up the actual causes.

Sources B and C both acknowledge that religion was a cause of the unrest, but neither suggest it was the main cause. Source C argues that the rebels wanted the return of the mass and the religious situation restored to the position it was at Henry VIII's death, and this is supported by the final demands of the Western rebels. However, the ambassador's report does not distinguish between the different rebellions and their causes but writes more generally as he also comments that some rebellions were due to enclosure, which was certainly true of the unrest in East Anglia, where the rising began with enclosures being pulled down. His understanding of the causes is therefore supported by the rebel demands and, as he is reporting to the Senate in Venice as ambassador, his role would be to report the actual events. Source B also suggests that religion was a cause of the unrest but, as the source suggests, religious demands did not dominate. As the source is the demands of the rebels it is likely to reflect their demands and the concern about the loss of common land was genuine in East Anglia as a number of gentry had put large flocks of sheep on common land on which many peasants depended upon for grazing their own sheep. It is also not surprising that they complained about rents as prices were rising quickly in this period and many were unable to afford the rises. The final complaint about the gentry and their behaviour is reflected in other demands about rabbit warrens and both their behaviour in local government and the attacks made on them during the rising and at Mousehold Heath, where some were put on trial. Source B does suggest there were religious concerns, but unlike Source A, the demands were for greater reform and this is further supported by their actions at Mousehold as they brought in Protestant preachers. Both Sources B and C therefore appear to be valid in their interpretation of the causes as they are supported by rebel demands and also their actions.

Side annotations:

The response establishes an overview of the sources in relation to the question. Such a start suggests that the response will be source driven and that the candidate has a clear understanding of each source about the issue in the question.

Own knowledge is directly linked to the source to explain why the view it offers can be seen to be valid.

Further knowledge is applied, but there is a balanced discussion about the limits to the value of the rebels' demands.

The provenance is considered and a good link is made to Source D and an explanation offered as to why Somerset's view appears to have changed.

The response deals with Sources B and C together as they both suggest that religion was a cause, if not the main or only cause.

Both sources are evaluated using both their provenance and own knowledge to reach a judgement about them in relation to the question.

Source D plays down the role of religion, and although written again by Somerset is in contrast to Source A. However, although Somerset is correct to stress the social and economic causes of unrest, with attacks on enclosures and the gentry seen in much of the country, he is wrong to dismiss religion as it played a role in the West Country, Yorkshire and Oxfordshire. His playing down of its role is because his position of Lord Protector was under attack and he was blamed by many of the ruling class for encouraging unrest by his policies, including the religious ones. By the end of August, with his position weakening, having had to call on Northumberland and Russell to suppress the risings in East Anglia and the west, as well as abandoning his policy in Scotland, he was trying to bolster his own position and therefore suggested that the religious change was not a genuine cause of unrest, but instead was exploited by Catholic priests to cause disquiet. Although there may be some validity in this view, as seen in the changing nature of the demands of the Western rebels, Somerset's view is coloured by his attempt to preserve his own position and deflect criticism, as he had accepted that religion was an issue in Source A.

Once again, detailed own knowledge and provenance are used to evaluate the source.

The sources do support the view that religion was a cause of unrest, but only Source A suggests that it was the main cause. The other sources suggest that social and economic causes were at least as important, if not more, than religion and that the scale of social unrest in much of central, eastern and southern England would suggest that view has much validity.

Although the judgement is brief, it is based on the sources and not own knowledge.

All the sources are evaluated using both own knowledge and their provenance. The own knowledge is directly linked to the sources and the response does not simply provide lots of knowledge about the unrest of 1549, but uses it to support or challenge the views offered in the sources. The issue of provenance might have been developed, but the response avoids the use of 'stock' comments and instead comments on developments that had taken place in England to explain why a particular view, as in Source D, might be offered. The answer remains focused on the question and addresses the question as to whether religion was the main cause. It therefore addresses all the issues required to reach the higher levels.

Considering provenance

Rewrite the answer so that the provenance of the sources is considered in more detail but avoids using just stock comments.

Glossary

Acts of Attainder   An Act of Parliament which declares a person guilty of treason and the loss of all their property to the Crown.

Amicable Grant   An additional tax Wolsey demanded in 1525 to fund Henry's expedition to France. It resulted in large-scale unrest in East Anglia and widespread non-payment.

Auld Alliance   The affectionate name given to the alliance between France and Scotland which started in 1295 and was signed by all Scottish and French monarchs, except Louis XI. The alliance had begun as a result of Edward I's military success against the Scots and the likelihood of their complete defeat. It continued until 1560.

Benevolences   Forced loans that would not be repaid.

Civil law   A legal system concerned with the private relations of the community. It was the system that dominated Europe and was based on Roman law.

Common law   Law that is derived from custom and precedent.

Commonwealth writers   A group of writers who were concerned that the social order was being neglected as landowners ignored the concepts of justice and charity.

Debasement   The reduction in the amount of silver content in the coins.

Dowry   The money or property paid by the father of the bride on her marriage.

Enclosure   Landowners put hedges around their fields, often changing land use from crops to sheep farming. Some landowners also seized land that had been used by the community (common land) which had been used by the peasantry for grazing sheep.

Excommunication   The Pope had the power to debar anyone from receiving the Holy Communion, which implied they were cut off from the Church.

English staple   A place where English companies had the exclusive right to buy and sell goods.

Faction   Self-interested groups around the King/Queen.

Foldcourse system   A system by which sheep and cattle are allowed onto land where crops were grown in order to fertilise it.

French pension   An annual pension of approximately £5,000 per year paid to the English King by France.

Heresy   Religious beliefs that departed from the official Catholic doctrine.

Hundred Years War   Term used to describe the wars between England and France that took place between 1337 and 1453.

Hunne Case   Richard Hunne was a Londoner who refused to pay the fee charged by the Church on the death of his son. He was sued by the Church and won, but they retaliated, using praemunire. He was arrested by Church authorities, and later found dead in suspicious circumstances while in Church custody. The Church was blamed for his death and historians have used the incident to show the corrupt nature of the Church.

Justice of the Peace (JP)   Local government officer responsible for maintaining order and implementing legislation in their county.

King's Council   The King's Council was another term for the Privy Council, a permanent and hand-picked group of advisors.

Lancastrian   A member or supporter of the royal house of Lancaster; before Henry VII the last Lancastrian king had been Henry VI. It was his reign (1422–61 and 1470–71) that saw the conflict with the house of York, known as the Wars of the Roses start.

Legatus a latere   A legate granted full papal powers to deal with a specific issue away from Rome.

Litany   A series of responses used in church services.

Order of the Garter   An order of knighthood introduced by Edward III, it became the highest order of chivalry.

Papal dispensation   The written permission of the Pope allowing a person to get married, often to a close relative, or to divorce.

Papal legate   A representative of the Pope who has been given papal powers.

Pluralism   The practice of clergymen holding more than one parish.

Praemunire   A law that made the introduction of any papal law into the country illegal.

Prorogue   A monarch had the right to suspend a parliamentary session until further notice.

Regency Council   A group of ministers, usually of nobles and landed gentry, who ruled on behalf of the king until he comes of age.

Retainers   The small professional, private army of a noble, they wore the uniforms of the noble they served.

Royal rights   The rights that the King could claim over people, it included his rights due to the feudal system and the King being at the head of the social ladder.

Seminaries   Training colleges for Roman Catholic priests.

Standing army   A regular army, regularly recruited and employed, England did not have one because it could not afford it and later it was seen as a threat to liberty.

Standish affair   A dispute in which Friar Standish, supported by parliament, attacked the privileges of the clergy and was therefore unpopular with bishops. It led to a debate about the power of the Church and State.

Suffragan   A bishop who was appointed to help a bishop with a diocese; a deputy.

Transubstantiation   The belief that during the mass or Eucharist the bread and wine are transformed into the body and blood of Christ.

Treaty of Étaples   Peace treaty signed with France in 1492. The French agreed not to aid English rebels, pay the arrears from the Treaty of Picquigny and pay most of Henry's expenses in Brittany.

Treaty of Picquigny   Signed in 1475 between the King of France and Edward IV, by which the French paid the English to remove their armies from French soil. This was known as the French pension and was renewed under Henry VII.

Visitation   An inspection by a bishop or archbishop of his diocese or archbishopric to look into clerical standards and the state of church buildings.

Wars of the Roses   The wars between the two royal houses of Lancaster and York that lasted from the 1450s until Henry VII's victory at Bosworth, although some have said they ended only with Henry's victory over Lambert Simnel in 1486.

Yorkist   A member or supporter of the house of York, the supporters backed the claim to the English throne of the descendants of Edward IV and Richard III.

Key figures

Catherine of Aragon (1485–1536)   The daughter of Ferdinand of Aragon and Isabella of Castile. She married Henry VII's eldest son, Arthur, but he died in 1502. Henry VII kept her in England after Arthur's death and permission was obtained from the Pope for her to marry Henry VII's other son. The marriage did not take place until Henry VIII came to the throne. Although she had a number of children, only Mary Tudor survived, and her last pregnancy was in 1518. By the mid 1520s Henry had stopped sleeping with her. His attempts to divorce her dominated the second half of the 1520s, but it was made more difficult because of the international situation and Catherine's refusal to agree. The divorce was granted by Cranmer, who ruled the marriage invalid. Catherine was popular in England and maintained support even after her fall.

Anne Boleyn (c.1507–36)   Anne Boleyn was the younger daughter of Thomas Boleyn. She was sent to France at the age of twelve, but returned in 1522 and joined the English court. Her sister was one of Henry VIII's mistresses and he determined to make her his mistress also, but she refused. She insisted on marriage; by the end of 1532 she was pregnant and was secretly married to the King at the start of 1533. As Queen she promoted her own family, but her failure to give Henry a male heir led to her execution in 1536 on grounds of adultery.

Margaret of Burgundy (1446–1503)   She was the sister of Edward IV and Richard III. Married to Charles the Bold of Burgundy, she allowed her court to become the centre of Yorkist plots against Henry VII. She provided financial and military support for Lambert Simnel and Perkin Warbeck.

Thomas Cranmer (1489–1556)   His career began as an academic at Cambridge until he came to notice with his views about Henry VIII's divorce. He was dramatically promoted to be Archbishop of Canterbury and worked with Cromwell to bring about the Reformation. He married the niece of a Lutheran minister, but kept the matter quiet. He was responsible for many of the Protestant reforms under Edward VI, most notably the Prayer Books, but was arrested soon after Mary came to the throne and was eventually burnt in 1556 for his beliefs.

Thomas Cromwell (c.1485–1540)   Cromwell was the son of an ale-house keeper. In his youth he fought for the French army before he then turned to trade and travelled widely. He later took service with Wolsey and became an MP. From 1531 he was in the royal service, becoming the King's Secretary and Vicar-General. He drafted the acts of the Reformation Parliament, including the Dissolution, and also carried out reforms to the administration of government in the 1530s. However, the failure of the Cleves marriage led to his fall and execution in 1540.

Edward VI (1537–53)   The only legitimate surviving male son of Henry VIII, his mother, Jane Seymour, died in childbirth. Usually seen as a sickly child, this was not true; it was only in the last months of his life he became ill, probably with tuberculosis, and died in July 1553. He had a humanist and Protestant education, which influenced his religious beliefs. He was a very intelligent child and this led to him taking a great interest in government, but particularly religion. He was certainly influential in some of the religious changes in his reign and played a role in trying to prevent his Catholic half-sister, Mary Tudor, from inheriting the throne through the Devise.

Stephen Gardiner (c.1482–1555)   Gardiner was educated at Cambridge and became Bishop of Winchester in 1531. Although Catholic in his beliefs, he supported the royal headship of the Church. His conservative religious view led to his imprisonment under Edward, but was appointed Lord Chancellor under Mary. He wanted Mary to marry Courtenay, supported the burnings of Protestants and wanted Elizabeth to be executed. He died in 1555, which allowed William Paget to dominate.

Henry VII (1457–1509)   He was the son of Edmund Tudor and Margaret Beaufort. His mother was descended from John of Gaunt and this gave Henry Tudor a claim, through the Lancastrians, to the throne, which he gained by force, killing Richard III at Bosworth. Henry restored law and order after the Wars of the Roses, but is often remembered for his harsh financial policies, which restored the power of the Crown. He helped to end the Wars of the Roses by his marriage to Elizabeth of York and by defeating a series of Yorkist claimants. He established the Tudor dynasty which ruled England until Elizabeth I's death in 1603.

Henry VIII (1491–1547)   The second son of Henry VII and Elizabeth of York, it was only the earlier death of his elder brother, Arthur, that brought Henry to the throne when his father died. He also married his dead brother's wife, Catherine of Aragon, which would lead to later difficulties, as she failed to produce a male heir; efforts to resolve the problem led to the break from the Catholic Church. A true Renaissance prince, he loved music, theology, jousting and hawking, as well as warfare. He is also remembered both for having six wives and his expanding girth!

Lady Jane Grey (1537–54)   She was the great-granddaughter of Henry VII and first cousin once removed of Edward VI. Her parents were the Duke of Suffolk and Lady Frances Brandon. She married Guildford Dudley, the son of the Duke of Northumberland and Edward's Lord President of the Council, against her wishes. In June 1553 Edward VI, through the Devise, named her as his heir to prevent the throne passing to his Catholic half-sister, Mary Tudor. Jane was very reluctantly crowned Queen, but lasted for only nine days before Mary took the throne. She was imprisoned and charged with treason, but initially her life was spared. However, following Wyatt's rebellion in 1554 she was executed.

Thomas More (1478–1535)   More was a trained lawyer, but built up a reputation as a leading humanist. He was appointed Lord Chancellor after Wolsey's fall. However, he disagreed with Henry VIII over his divorce. Henry demanded More take the oath of succession, but More refused and was sent to the Tower. In 1535 perjured evidence was used to get him convicted of treason and he was condemned to death.

Duke of Northumberland (1504–53)   He was the son of John Dudley, whom Henry VIII executed as a scapegoat for Henry VII's financial measures. In 1542 he became Viscount Lisle and gained a military reputation. On Henry VIII's death he was made Earl of Warwick and Lord Great Chamberlain. In 1549 he put down Kett's rebellion and was then involved in the autumn intrigue that led to Somerset's fall and eventually his appointment as Lord President of the Council in January 1550. However, in 1553 he was involved in the plan to alter the succession in favour of Lady Jane Grey, but its failure and his own involvement resulted in his trial and execution.

William Paget (1506–63)   Paget was appointed Principal Secretary of State in 1543 and played a major role in government until his death in 1563. He worked for three monarchs during the period, and was appointed a peer in 1550. He opposed Gardiner and supported the Spanish marriage, but was opposed to the persecution and advised Mary against executing Elizabeth after the Wyatt rebellion. His political career ended in 1558 when he was not asked to join Elizabeth's Council.

Cardinal Pole (1500–58)   Pole was of royal and Yorkist blood; his mother was the Countess of Salisbury. He was educated for the priesthood, but on opposing Henry VIII's divorce he went into exile. His mother was executed for treason in 1541. Pole became a cardinal and on Mary's accession was appointed legate to England, and then Archbishop of Canterbury. His arrival was delayed because of the argument over former monastic lands. In 1557 his legateship was removed and he was ordered to return to Rome on charges of heresy, but Mary refused to allow him to leave. He continued in office until his death on the same day as Mary.

Lambert Simnel (c. 1477–c1535)   An Oxford priest, Richard Symonds passed off his ten-year-old pupil initially as Richard, Duke of York, the youngest of the Princes in the Tower. However, he changed his mind when rumours circulated about the death of the Earl of Warwick and Simnel was passed off as him. He was taken to Ireland, where there was much Yorkist support, and crowned as Edward VI. With support from Margaret of Burgundy and Ireland a force was raised and landed in England in 1487. Defeated at East Stoke, Simnel was put to work in the royal kitchens.

Duke of Somerset (c.1506–52)   He was the brother of Henry VIII's third wife, Jane Seymour, and uncle of Edward VI. He became a member of the Privy Council in 1537 and in the 1540s gained experience as a diplomat and soldier, leading the army in Scotland. After Henry's death he was appointed Lord Protector and was given sovereign authority until Edward was eighteen. He was made Duke of Somerset in 1547, but his arrogance and failure to control the unrest in 1549 led to his dismissal from office and imprisonment. Although he was released and returned to the Council in 1550, he was accused of plotting to overthrow Northumberland and was tried and executed in 1552.

Mary Tudor (1516–58) The eldest daughter of Henry VIII through his marriage to the Spanish princess, Catherine of Aragon, Mary was declared illegitimate following her parents' divorce. Throughout the religious changes of both her father's and half-brother's reigns she remained a devout Catholic, despite pressures to conform. Although initially denied the throne by the Devise, she acted quickly to defeat Northumberland and take the throne. Perhaps driven by her Spanish ancestry, she married Philip II of Spain in 1554, but despite a series of phantom pregnancies, she remained childless and upon her death in 1558 the throne passed to her half-sister, Elizabeth. She is probably best remembered for returning England to Catholicism and the burning of nearly 300 Protestants who would not conform.

Perkin Warbeck (c.1475–99) A young Flemish boy, but with Yorkist backing, he impersonated Richard, the younger son of Edward IV. He was taken to Ireland by his employer, but most Irish refused to back him. He then went to France, Burgundy and then the court of the Emperor. His attempt to invade England in 1495 failed and he fled to Scotland and married the King's cousin. However, following peace with England he was forced to flee again to Ireland, but was again rejected and so attempted another invasion of England, which again failed and he was arrested, sent to the Tower and later executed after an escape attempt.

Thomas Wolsey (c.1472–1530) The son of an Ipswich butcher, he graduated from Oxford and ordained a priest in 1498. He became almoner at Henry VII's court and then royal chaplain. He rose to prominence under Henry VIII, joining the Council in 1510. He provided Henry with the army to invade France in 1513. In 1514 he was made Archbishop of York, cardinal and Lord Chancellor in 1515 and papal legate in 1518. He was Henry's Chief Minister until his failure to obtain a divorce for Henry and was removed from power in 1529.

Timeline

1485	August	Battle of Bosworth
	October	Henry VII crowned King
1486	January	Marriage of Henry VII to Elizabeth of York
		Commercial treaty with Brittany
	July	Conspiracy of Lovell and Stafford
	September	Birth of Prince Arthur
		Act of Resumption
1487	June	Simnel's rising and Battle of Stoke
		Renewal of treaty with Maximilian, heir to the Holy Roman Empire
1489	February	Treaty of Redon with Brittany
	March	Treaty of Medina del Campo with Spain
		Yorkshire rebellion
1491–99		Warbeck's rebellion
1491	June	Birth of Prince Henry
1492	November	Treaty of Étaples with France
1493		Cloth trade embargo with Netherlands
1495–96		Henry joins League of Venice
1496	February	Magnus Intercursus with Burgundy
1497	May	Cornish rising
1497	October	Warbeck surrenders
1499	November	Warbeck hanged
1501	November	Marriage of Arthur and Catherine of Aragon
1502	January	Peace of Ayton (Perpetual Peace) with Scotland
	April	Death of Prince Arthur
1503	February	Death of Queen Elizabeth
	August	Marriage of Margaret to James IV of Scotland
1506	April	Edmund de la Pole imprisoned in the Tower
		Malus Intercursus with Burgundy
1508	December	League of Cambrai
1509	April	Death of Henry VII
	June	Henry VIII marries Catherine of Aragon
1513	August	Battle of the Spurs
	September	Defeat of Scots at Flodden Field
1514		Wolsey becomes Chief Minister
1515	September	Wolsey made a cardinal
	November	Wolsey appointed Lord Chancellor
1516	February	Mary Tudor born
1518	May	Wolsey appointed papal legate
	October	Treaty of London
1520	June	Field of Cloth of Gold
1521	August	Wolsey met Francis I at Calais
	August	Wolsey met Charles V at Bruges
1525	April	Amicable Grant
	August	Treaty of the More with France
1526	January	Eltham Ordinances
1527	May	Wolsey instructed to explore the possibility of a divorce
1529	October	Wolsey removed from power
	November	Reformation Parliament called
1532	December	Anne Boleyn becomes pregnant
1533	January	Henry marries Anne in secret
	February	Act in Restraint of Appeals
1534	November	Act of Supremacy
1536	February	Act for the Dissolution of the Smaller Monasteries
	July	Ten Articles
	October	Pilgrimage of Grace
1538	June	Peace between France and Spain leads to invasion fear
1539	April	Publication of the Great Bible
	June	Six Articles
1540	Jan–Jul	Henry's marriage to, and divorce from, Anne of Cleves
	July	Thomas Cromwell executed
	July	Henry's marriage to Catherine Howard
1542	February	Execution of Catherine Howard
	November	Battle of Solway Moss
1543	February	Alliance with Charles V
	May	King's Book
	July	Henry's marriage to Catherine Parr

1544	September	Invasion of France, Boulogne captured
1546	December	Henry drafts his last will
1547	January	Death of Henry VIII
		Regency Council established, Somerset Lord Protector
	July	Book of Homilies and royal injunctions
	November	Dissolution of the Chantries
1548	February	Images to be removed
	April	Murder of William Body, Helston
	June	Commission of enquiry to investigate enclosure
	Summer	Rural riots
		Council object to Somerset's policies and Enclosure Commission
	December	First Book of Common Prayer
1549	January	First Act of Uniformity
	May	Unrest Hampshire, Somerset, Wiltshire
	June	New Prayer book introduced
		Western or Prayer Book rebellion starts
	July	Kett's rebellion and uprisings in Yorkshire, Northamptonshire, Bedfordshire, Oxfordshire and Buckinghamshire
	August	Exeter relieved by Lord John Russell
		Defeat of Western rebels at Sampford Courtenay
		Defeat of Kett at Dussindale
	October	Coup removes Somerset
1549–50		Struggle to control Privy Council
1550	January	New Ordinal
	February	Northumberland becomes Lord President of the Council

	November	Stone altars to be replaced with wooden tables
1552	January	Execution of Somerset
		Second Book of Common Prayer
	April	Second Book of Uniformity
	November	Forty-Two Articles
1553	May	Northumberland's son marries Lady Jane Grey
	June	Devise to exclude Mary Tudor
	July	Edward VI dies, Lady Jane Grey proclaimed Queen
		Mary Tudor defeats Lady Jane Grey and becomes Queen
	August	Northumberland executed
	September	Arrest of Cranmer, Latimer, Hooper and Ridley
		Act of Repeal
1554	January	Wyatt's rebellion
	February	Wyatt arrested, Elizabeth imprisoned
	March	Royal injunctions
	April	Heresy Laws passed
	July	Mary marries Philip of Spain
	November	Pole returns, Second Act of Repeal, end of excommunication
1555	February	John Rogers first Protestant martyr
	October	Latimer and Ridley burned for heresy
	December	Pole appointed Archbishop of Canterbury, Cranmer deprived
1556	March	Cranmer burned
1557	June	Pole recalled to Rome on charges of heresy, Mary refuses to allow him to go
1558	November	Death of Mary Tudor and Pole

Answers

Page 9

Turning assertion into argument

- Henry's marriage was important in strengthening his position on the throne **because it united the houses of York and Lancaster.**
- People were tired of the instability caused by the Wars of the Roses **and were therefore willing to support him if he could bring stability.**
- The death of Richard at Bosworth strengthened Henry's position **as there few surviving Yorkists around whom opposition could rally.**
- The Yorkists were weak **and therefore had to use Pretenders to try and take the throne**.
- Henry's skills allowed him to strengthen his position **as he dated his reign from the day before Bosworth so he could declare anyone who fought against him a traitor and seize their lands.**

Page 11

Spot the mistake

There are a number of mistakes. There were few Yorkists left to claim the throne, hence the reliance on Pretenders. Henry did not easily defeat Simnel.

Page 13

Support or challenge?

Statement	Support	Challenge
The use of the Order of the Garter was seen as prestigious		x
The number of bonds and recognisances issued during his reign was particularly high	x	
Those who served him loyally were rewarded with patronage		x
Heavy fines were imposed on some nobles, with Lord Burgavenny paying over £70,000	x	
Henry reclaimed royal land through the Act of Resumption		x
The number of Acts of Attainder was causing disquiet	x	
There were fears that civil war might restart because of his policies	x	
His son's actions on taking the throne	x	

Introducing an argument

A possible paragraph might be:

Henry was at least partially successful in managing the nobility through the use of inducements and by giving a number of nobles who had fought against him at Bosworth a second chance. He also rewarded those who showed loyalty through patronage and involvement in Councils. However, he also antagonised many through his harsh financial measures, such as bonds and recognisances and use of attainders, which meant many were in debt to him. He limited the numbers of retainers they could keep and exploited his feudal rights over them. This has led some to argue that he failed in his policy as many nobles were on the verge of rebellion by the end of his reign.

Page 15

Delete as applicable

Henry VII's financial policy was a great success to a **fair extent**. He was able to increase **some** areas of ordinary revenue. He was particularly **unsuccessful** with customs which **decreased** in comparison to the reign of Edward IV. His exploitation of revenue from crown lands was a **fair** success and this was **similar to** his exploitation of the justice system. However, raising money through extraordinary revenue was **less** successful as he was expected to use it **in times of emergencies** and using this method was **unpopular** and it provided a **variable** income.

Identify an argument

Sample 1 contains the argument.

Page 17

Complete the paragraph

The restoration of law and order in the counties was difficult because it had broken down during the Wars of Roses. Henry needed to ensure that his laws were enforced in the localities, but this was not always easy. This point is supported by his reliance on unpaid officials. The use of JPs was not new, but Henry increased their role and this now included imposing economic and social laws and dispensing justice. However, they were unpaid officials and were concerned that they did not become unpopular in the localities, but by choosing men from the second rank of society they were more likely to be loyal and carry out the king's wishes. Despite their role, Henry still needed the support of the nobility to ensure that laws were implemented in the localities and regional councils to enforce law and order in the peripheral regions were equally important. Thus the explanation cannot be totally one-sided.

Page 21

Eliminate irrelevance

Henry had numerous foreign policy aims and his policy can be divided into three distinct phases. In the first part of his reign from 1485 to 1492 Henry's main concern was to secure his throne. ~~During this period he followed a policy of diplomacy in order to win support, while at home he also tried to eliminate those who could~~ threaten ~~his throne, crushing unrest and limiting the power of the nobility.~~ In the period from 1493 to 1502 it appears that Henry's main concern was to secure peace with Scotland, which was done through the Treaty of Ayton. This also helped him to secure his throne as it helped in the defeat of Warbeck. In the last period of Henry's reign his aim was to ensure that he was not isolated overseas as England was still relatively weak. ~~He was also faced with a declining position at home with the death of his wife and eldest son, so his aim at home was to ensure the Tudor dynasty survived.~~

Page 23

You're the examiner

The paragraph would reach at least Level 5 as there is consistent focus, argument and a judgement, which is developed.

Page 25

Complete the paragraph

The Treaty of Medina del Campo was a reflection of Henry's concern to obtain foreign recognition and that he needed the support of major European powers in order to secure the Tudor dynasty on the throne, which was still threatened by Pretenders, such as Perkin Warbeck, which could threaten the King's position. The treaty included an agreement that Spain would not support other claimants to the English throne. Henry wanted to secure a valuable marriage for his son, which would strengthen England's position within Europe and stop them from appearing to be a second-rate power, which had been their position since the ending of the Hundred Years War with France. The treaty would also signify that Ferdinand and Isabella of Spain considered Henry secure enough on the throne to allow their daughter to marry into the Tudor family. The treaty also contained trade clauses and Henry hoped that these would give England access to lucrative markets. The importance of the treaty can be explained both in terms of recognition for the Tudors and strengthening English security, and improving trade **and was therefore particularly important to Henry as it**

helped him to achieve one of his most important foreign policy aims of gaining recognition for the Tudor dynasty from a major European power.

Page 27

The flaw in the argument

The flaw in the argument is that the opening sentence is contradicted in the main body of the essay. The paragraph could be improved by ensuring the supporting detail supports the opening sentence or the opening sentence is changed to support the detail in the paragraph.

Turning assertion into argument

Henry VII's marriage agreement with Spain was successful in increasing dynastic security **because it brought the Tudor dynasty recognition from a major power**.

However, the success was only short-lived because **Arthur died and the attempt to arrange a marriage with his other son did not occur during his lifetime**.

Similarly the marriage agreement with Scotland was only partially successful because **it did not end border skirmishes and full-scale war broke out under Henry VIII**.

Page 29

Spot the mistake

The mistake is that the answer is just a list of Henry's foreign policy aims. In order to reach at least Level 5 there would need to be some developed judgement as to the relative importance of foreign policy aims.

Introducing an argument

Possible opening paragraph:

Although many of Henry's treaties with other nations included clauses relating to trade as this would help to improve both his and the nation's finances, it was not his major concern and therefore he was willing to sacrifice trade when national security was threatened, as happened with Burgundy and their support for Yorkists. Moreover, England was not particularly strong and this made it difficult to negotiate beneficial trade deals with other states.

Possible conclusion:

There were occasions where trade was improved and treaties signed by Henry did widen the scope of English trade in the Mediterranean. However, it was always secondary to national security as was seen in the dealings with Burgundy and the difficulties of improving English trade was also seen in the dealings with Hanse. Therefore, although Henry attempted to improve trade to increase his revenue, the concern over security and English weakness made it more difficult.

Page 33

Develop the detail

Henry wanted to break from the past and the rule of his father **as the latter years of Henry VII's reign had been characterised by harshness and meanness.** He was able to demonstrate this in a number of different policy areas. Henry distanced himself from his father in terms of his father's harsh financial measures **by arresting and executing Empson and Dudley who had implemented the policies.** His father had also relied a great deal on 'new men' but Henry restored the traditional alliance with the nobility through his policies **of creating new nobles, lavish spending and establishing a vibrant court.** Whereas his father had come close to civil war with them by the end of his reign, Henry VIII was able to win their support. The most important way he did this was through his foreign policy, which was very different from that of his father **as Henry went to war with France in 1512 and 1513, which also kept the nobles occupied and showed Henry's chivalrous nature.** In order to achieve this break he had to ignore the advice of some of his father's advisors**, such as Warham and Fox,** who had been keen to uphold the old policy. Not only in this area, but Henry VIII also showed a break with the past through his marriage **as he soon married Catherine of Aragon after his father had refused to return her to Spain after Arthur's death and kept her virtual prisoner.**

Page 35

Support or challenge?

	Support	Challenge
The Scots were defeated at the Battle of Flodden		x
Henry VIII captured Therouanne and Tournai and defeated the French at the Battle of the Spurs		x
The Treaty of London was a diplomatic triumph		x
The Field of Cloth of Gold brought little gain and was costly	x	
The marriage of Mary to Louis XII and then the Duke of Suffolk	x	
War with France in 1523	x	
England's alliances with France with the Treaty of the More and Westminster	x	
The diplomatic attempts to get Henry's marriage to Catherine of Aragon annulled	x	

Turning assertion into argument

Henry VIII's foreign policy was successful only in the short term **because he lacked the financial resources and alliances to sustain a long-term campaign.**

Henry was able to achieve some glory through his policies **as he was able to make England diplomatically important with the Treaty of London.**

However, he was unable to achieve either of his main goals **as alliances soon broke down and he lacked the money to launch a full-scale invasion of France.**

Page 37

Delete as applicable

Wolsey's domestic policies were successful to a **fair extent.** The changes made to the legal system brought about **great** benefits for the poorer members of society as justice was **more available** to them. The number of cases dealt with by courts **increased.** Wolsey's financial policy was also **mostly successful** as the amount of money he raised for the King **increased.** His greatest **success** was the introduction of the subsidy, but his attempts to raise money in the 1520s to finance war against France were **less successful.** Wolsey's social policies were **unpopular** with the nobility who **disliked** his attack on enclosure, however, Wolsey **abandoned** this policy. Throughout the period Wolsey's relationship with the nobility was **a failure,** in part this might have been because of his background but also because many of his policies **attacked** them.

Complete the paragraph

Wolsey was able to increase the amount of money that he brought in to fund Henry's ambitious and expensive foreign policy. An important development was the introduction of the subsidy, which became the standard parliamentary tax and replaced the old fifteenth and tenth. The government now had a system that was based on the realistic assessment of wealth. This resulted in a considerable increase in the amount of wealth generated, but in the 1520s was still not enough to fund an invasion of France and forced Wolsey to resort to a non-parliamentary tax, the Amicable Grant, which caused unrest in East Anglia. Another major consequence was that this failure reduced Henry's confidence in Wolsey and may have encouraged further noble opposition towards him as they saw his position was less secure. Wolsey raised in excess of £800,000 for Henry but it did not cover the £1.7 million that was spent on war. **Therefore, although Wolsey was able to dramatically increase the amount of money available to Henry for warfare it was simply not enough to meet the demands of a King whose job Wolsey's was to serve and was therefore at best a limited success.**

Page 39

Introducing an argument

Possible introduction:

Although there were some complaints and grumblings about the Church in the period before the Reformation, these were limited. Instead what emerges is a picture of a Church that was thriving with financial support for buildings and guilds being provided by ordinary people, ordination rates still high and religious literature still popular.

Possible conclusion:

Although there were some complaints, which is hardly surprising given the size of the Church and its wealth, most people appeared to be satisfied by it. There was little evidence of opposition and, on the contrary, many were still investing large sums in it, hardly suggesting that it was unpopular.

Page 41

Identify an argument

Sample 2 contains the argument.

Develop the detail

Wolsey had resisted attacks on his position for many years over a number of issues, **such as the Amicable Grant and his use of justice to attack the nobility,** and had been able to withstand criticism from groups, **most notably the nobility,** who disliked him, at least in part because of his background, **being the son of an Ipswich butcher.** This would suggest that the failure to gain Henry a divorce was the most important reason. Wolsey also faced factional opposition **from the Boleyns** and they blamed him for being deliberately slow. There may have been some truth in this, **as Wolsey had nothing to gain from the divorce as Anne was more involved in politics and would lessen his influence** and they put pressure on the King to abandon Wolsey. The situation for Wolsey had become very difficult by 1529 **as Anne refused to be Henry's mistress and he urgently needed a male heir** and the King was no longer willing to wait for his chief minister to achieve the divorce.

Page 45

Turning assertion into argument

Most of the early changes had little impact on religious beliefs **as they concerned England's relationship with Rome and therefore had little impact on doctrine.**

There were some doctrinal changes in the 1530s that suggested a move towards Protestantism, **most notably the attack on purgatory with the Dissolution and the Act of Ten Articles which rejected four Catholic sacraments.**

However, given Henry's religious views and his policies in the period from 1539–43, England remained Catholic because **the King did not abandon his belief in transubstantiation and Thomas Cromwell, who had** probably been the driving force behind any moves towards Protestantism, had fallen from power.

Develop the detail

Henry's personal views were very important in influencing religious developments. This was particularly true once he had removed his Chief Minister, **Thomas Cromwell,** who had pursued a more Protestant line. Henry was very traditional in many of his religious beliefs, **most notably upholding transubstantiation and his belief in purgatory** and punished those who disagreed with his views, **executing John Lambert in 1538 for denying transubstantiation.** As a result, any moves towards Protestant views over the Eucharist were resisted and an **Act of Six Articles** was passed in 1539, which upheld Catholic views. The King was also concerned about who should have access to the Bible and introduced legislation, **the 1543 Act for the Advancement of True Religion,** on that despite earlier legislation **in 1538** that had made the Bible available in churches. Henry had also refused to support the Bishop's Book, which attacked some Catholic practices but did back a more conservative publication, **the King's Book,** in 1543. Even his marriage in 1540 **to Catherine Howard** suggests that he wanted to uphold traditional beliefs.

Page 47

Support or challenge?

	Support	Challenge
The 1535 Valor Ecclesiasticus revealed how wealthy the monasteries were	x	
Visitations showed that the monasteries were in a poor spiritual condition		x
Cromwell had promised to make Henry the richest man in Christendom	x	
Monks had been leading opponents of the religious changes		x
Monasteries had been closed in other Protestant areas, such as Scandinavia		x
Monasteries upheld traditional religious beliefs		x
Henry gained a lot of land from the Dissolution which he could use as rewards	x	
Henry needed money to build defences against a possible Catholic crusade	x	

Delete as appropriate

The size of the Pilgrimage of Grace meant that the rising was a **serious** threat to Henry as he was able to raise a **smaller** force than the rebels. The rebels were also able to gain support from a **wide** area in the north and were able to take important towns and castles. However, most of the rebels' demands were **religious** and this made it a **minor** threat to the king. Although the rebellion lasted **months** the King was able to **suppress** the rebels in early 1537.

Page 49

Complete the paragraph

Cromwell was closely associated with reformist beliefs and was probably instrumental in some of the Protestant legislation of the 1530s. This would undoubtedly have brought him into conflict with the conservative faction led by Bishop Stephen Gardiner and the Duke of Norfolk. They were able to entice Henry with Norfolk's niece, Catherine Howard, who appealed to Henry after his disastrous marriage to Anne of Cleves for which Cromwell had been responsible. Henry soon became infatuated with Catherine, who was portrayed as an attractive and innocent nineteen year old. **As a result the conservative faction was able to exploit the King's suspicions about Cromwell's religious beliefs and use Catherine as bait to increase their influence and bring about Cromwell's fall.**

Eliminate irrelevance

Cromwell's fall from power in 1540 was the result of many factors. ~~He had served Henry well and been the architect behind the measures that resulted in the break with Rome and had secured the Royal Supremacy, but this was similar to Cardinal Wolsey who achieved a great deal for Henry. Cromwell had probably achieved more for the King than any other royal servant, bringing about what has been described as a revolution in government and making Henry wealthy through the Dissolution.~~ Despite many achievements, he had alienated many among the nobility because of his background. His position was further weakened by factional struggles between the religious reformists, which Cromwell represented and the more Catholic faction under Norfolk and Gardiner, which emerged triumphant following the disastrous Cleves marriage, which Cromwell had been responsible for organising. Howard was also able to use his attractive niece, Catherine Howard, to woo Henry and persuade him to believe stories he was told about his Chief Minister.

Page 51

You're the examiner

The response would reach at least Level 5 as it is focused on the question and is consistently analytical with some developed judgement.

Page 57

Spot the inference

	I	P	S	X
Henry VIII's death caused unrest				x
There were concerns among the Council on how to achieve stability	x			
The late King's will was enforced and Somerset became Lord Protector			x	
Edward was proclaimed King when his father's death was announced, the Council enforced the King's will and appointed Somerset as Protector		x		

Page 61

Support or challenge?

Source A: Supports because it mentions they agreed with Mary's right to the title (of Queen).

Source B: Supports because it mentions the wicked plan to deprive the rightful queen, even though the writer disliked Catholicism.

Source C: Challenges as they backed her only once they had guarantees about religion.

Doing reliability well

Source A: The writer is relying on someone else's information and, given Foxe's views, he is looking to explain why Mary triumphed. Some of the information is correct as Northumberland had executed Somerset, but this was partly because Somerset continued to plot against him, which is not mentioned and thus again questions the reliability.

Source B: The writer is protecting his own position and that of his family's as, although they do not like Catholicism, they are willing to put legitimacy before religion in order to secure their own position; however, it accurately reflects the response of many and explains why Mary triumphed.

Source C: The source is written by John Foxe, who is biased as he wanted to portray Mary as not keeping her word as she broke her promise not to make any religious innovations.

Page 65

Support or challenge?

Source	Support	Challenge
A		x
B	x	
C	x	
D	x	x

Page 73

Spot the inference

	I	P	S	X
The main reasons why the introduction of Protestantism was slow were the lack of qualified clergy and legislation		x		
It would be difficult to make England a Protestant nation within a short period and everything possible needs to be done to encourage the government.	x			
There were moves towards Protestantism, encouraged by the government, who considered religious change a priority				x
Bucer is concerned that not only can't the bishops agree on doctrine, but there is a lack of qualified clergy who do little to help by reading services quickly			x	
The bishops state that they need parliamentary support to act but parliament has many other issues that need its attention			x	

Page 75

Doing reliability well

Source A: This is likely to be unreliable as Mary has a vested interest to reassure her subjects about her religious aims, having only just come to the throne in difficult circumstances.

Source B: The source is likely to be reliable as the writer, the Spanish ambassador, was an expert and was present at court so would be aware of the issues.

Source C: The source is written by the ambassador whose job it was to be informed about developments and convey them to Mary's husband, who was out of the country, and therefore he should be viewed as an expert whose job it was to provide accurate advice.

Source D: The source is biased as Foxe reflects his own views and wanted to show how much support there was for Protestantism and how brave the martyrs were.

Page 85

Spot the inference

	I	P	S	X
The risings have spread and could be a threat. The demands of the rebels are largely social and economic, with some unrealistic requests, but where handled well they can be put down quickly so are not a serious threat.	x			
The ambassador is saying that peasant revolts have spread to all parts of England. He says that the peasants want land to be leased to them at the same rate as it was under Henry VII. The riots in some areas ended when food was taxed at a reasonable price. He says religion is not a major cause of the unrest.		x		
The revolts are widespread and are caused by economic issues, such as rent and the taxes on foodstuffs, while religion is not a major cause. Some ended when the taxes on food were reduced.			x	
The revolts were less about social and economic issues and more about religion and political problems.				x

Assessing reliability

When was it written?	July 1549
Why would Dandolo be eager to report the unrest in England?	It was his duty to inform the Venetian government
Was it a private or a public document?	Public
Who would read the document?	The government of Venice
From your own knowledge, was this typical of the explanations given for the unrest in England?	Yes, there is evidence of enclosure unrest in East Anglia and many other parts of central and southern England

Page 89

Doing reliability well

Source A: The source is written by the Archbishop of Canterbury so it will be biased, hence his comment about papists reflects his views. He has a vested interest to portray the rebels in this way.

Source B: The source is written by Robert Kett and the leadership of the rebellion so they would know what their demands were and there would be no point in not telling the Privy Council if they hoped to achieve their aims.

Source C: The writer should be an expert; as ambassador it is his responsibility to know such details and report them to his government.

Source D: The source is written to protect Somerset's reputation. His position was weak following the scale of the unrest and he did not want to admit that his religious policies were in part to blame, hence he blames the unrest on 'the vilest sort of men'.

Page 93

Doing reliability well

Source A: As ambassador it was his job to provide Charles with accurate information about developments, particularly as his son, Philip, was to marry Mary and would be concerned about developments; this suggests it should be accurate.

Source B: The source is designed to protect Mary's position; she is rallying the people of London against Wyatt and therefore may not reveal the true cause of the rising, which was the marriage, and instead accuses the rebels of rising for religious purposes as this would attract less support.

Source C: Although it is a chronicle and outlines the actual events, the use of some language suggests political bias and may make it less reliable.